Disneyland for Military Families 2019

By Steve Bell

Copyrights and Trademarks

Published by Magic Shell Media
P.O. Box 33823 Dayton, OH 45433
© 2017-2019 Stephen Bell
ISBN: 978-0-9996374-5-6

This book is dedicated to all military families! It takes a great family to support the military member. Freedom isn't free and we all pay our dues in our own way.

Contents

Introduction

Welcome to Disneyland for Military Families!

Planning a Disneyland vacation can be a complex endeavor for any family. During your planning you'll make many decisions that will affect all aspects of your vacation. Throw in the complexities of a military deployment schedule or the many varied military deals and discounts which are available from multiple sources and it can become a daunting task.

Relax and take a deep calming breath. This book is here to help you navigate all of those complexities. This is the only Disneyland book ever written specifically for the military community. It will present to you all of the information required to make informed decisions on how to plan for and save as much as possible on your Disneyland vacation as a military family.

A Disney vacation has never been more affordable for military members and their families, whether you are Active Duty, Reserve, Guard, or Retired, there is a discount for you. Disney's Armed Forces Salute beats any general public discount and we've got a whole chapter dedicated entirely to the Salute!

This book has literally been 48 years in the making. The research and experience that has gone into this book started with my family's first visit to Walt Disney World in 1971, the year it first opened. That first trip was then followed by well over 60 visits (both single and multiday trips), three years of working for Disney World in the Magic Kingdom theme park, 30 years of using military discounts to save as much as possible on my family's Disney vacations, and over 18 years helping other military members plan for and save on their Disney vacations both at my military units and via my website MilitaryDisneyTips.com.

Disney Relaxation

A Disney vacation is a unique experience; in that it is so immersive that it is very easy to leave behind the everyday cares, worries, and stress of the outside world.

It's the perfect place for a military family to spend time together and think of nothing else. It's the ideal location for a pre-deployment getaway, for reconnecting after a deployment, or for a special treat for the kids while mom or dad is away.

I hope this book will be a very useful resource for you in your planning and decision making process.

Steve Bell

Overview

The chapters in this book are organized in a totally different order than any other book that cover the Disney parks!

This is because there is a large amount of military specific information to cover first which will affect all of the normal basics where all other books start. We focus first on things such as military discount availability and military schedules.

My intent is to give you the background information, which is important to our community first, followed by more general information, and then flow smoothly into the planning process while keeping the military info in mind.

This book is specifically targeted at military visitors especially the discounts available to them and provides a comprehensive explanation of all of the options available for military families. Ticket discounts, room discounts, dining discounts, merchandise, and other discounts are all covered.

There are many rules that go along with these discounts; you'll find them all here. Many are not published by Disney, or anywhere else for that matter, but have been gathered from both official Disney sources and human intelligence sources within the Disney cast.

This book will also give you an overview of everything that Disneyland has to offer. You'll get a brief overview of the theme parks, resorts, restaurants, and entertainment options. As we talk about these, any military specific information or discounts will be mentioned.

We'll be talking about the history of Disney's military discounts, how they've evolved over the years and what to expect in the future.

How This Book Is Organized

The four chapters following this one cover material applicable only to the military. Here we'll discuss the various discounts and options that are only available to our community.

Then we will discuss deciding when to go which has several special considerations that military families need to think about before getting to the point where the general public starts their planning.

We will then talk about your options to consider when deciding where to stay: Disney, non-Disney, on property and off property as well as what discounts are available at each.

Next we'll cover things to do at Disneyland, from the theme parks to entertainment, and shopping.

We'll also get to things like dining and transportation. In these chapters we'll cover military specific information as well as everything else.

A very important chapter is the one about Disney's new technology, like FastPass and the Disneyland Park App.

We'll cover information on disability access for the wounded warriors or retirees who might need to know what is available for them.

And then we'll wrap it all up with some Disney vacation tips and advice.

The 2019 Edition

This edition of Disneyland for Military Families was written to cover the time period of the 2018 and 2019 Disney Armed Forces Salutes.

Prices quoted in the book will be 2019 prices unless noted otherwise. We've done our best to be as accurate as possible, but you should verify prices yourself as they are subject to change by those who set them.

Every effort has been made at the time of publication to make the information presented in this book as accurate and comprehensive as possible. The Walt Disney Company constantly makes changes and is trying new things, so inevitably there will be some differences in details when you take your vacation.

Ready to jump in? Let's go...

First we are going to take a look at the history of Disney Military discounts and we'll see just how good we have it now!

1. Disney Military Discounts, a Brief History and Overview

What's This Chapter About?

In this chapter we'll talk about the long-term history of Disney Military Discounts, what it was like in the past and how good we have it now.

We'll go over how the military discounts available to the military community for their Disney vacations have changed over the years.

Military discounts, whether from Disney or other sources, are usually a very fluid situation that could change at any time, so we'll also touch on how things look for the future.

Tickets

I started my military career back in the early 80s (I retired just a few years ago) and as far back as I can remember in my career my base ticket office sold slightly discounted tickets for both Walt Disney World and Disneyland.

For the majority of my career these were all that was available for the military community and they really didn't save you very much. These tickets are still available today and depending on the length and options, you will only save between four and eight percent off of the regular gate ticket price.

Several times over the years Disney has offered specially priced or sometimes even free, tickets for the military member. A couple of examples of this are:

- After the first Gulf War, Disney World offered a free one-day ticket for military members.
- During the first half of 2002 due to the post 9/11 travel industry slowdown, they offered a free seven-day ticket for the member and 50% off tickets for up to five of their guests. As the travel industry recovered, Disney discontinued this special military offer.

After the 2002 offer, just the regular military discounted tickets were again all that was available until 2009, when Disney started what is called the Disney Armed Forces Salute. This new offer came after the economic downturn and travel industry slowdown which began in the fall of 2008.

Here is a brief history of the Salute Discounts since then:

- The first Salute began in January 2009 and was initially a partial year offer, which was then extended 3 times, eventually through the end of the year.
- January 2010 saw another 7-month long offer, which was then extended twice through the end of the 2010 Disney fiscal year.
- In October 2010, after a 22-day break, Disney offered the first full year-long offer (25 October 2010 – 28 September 2011).
- In April 2011 Disney made a surprise announcement that the ongoing offer would be extended through 28 September 2012, making it a 2-year long offer.
- September 2012, 2013, and 2014 each saw one year long renewals
- In June 2015 the 28 September 2014 – October 2015 offer was extended through just prior to Christmas 2015.
- On 24 September 2015 Disney switched to offering a Calendar Year Salute Offer for 2016. It ran from 3 January through 19 December.
- On 28 September 2016 Disney announced the 2017 Disney Armed Forces Salute.

- On 28 September 2017 Disney announced the new 2018 Disney Armed Forces Salute.
- On 27 September 2017 Disney announced the new 2019 Disney Armed Forces Salute.

This Military Salute offers highly discounted theme park tickets for military members and their guests. These tickets have very detailed rules and restrictions because of the huge savings they offer. These tickets are about half off of the regular gate price!

Each Salute offer normally runs for only a one-year long period. Each year the Salute requires a renewal in order to continue for another year.

For much more information about the Disney Armed Forces Salute you should check out the Disney Armed Forces Salute chapter as well as the Disneyland Tickets Chapter.

Rooms

Disney Resorts

Since 2009, Disney has offered highly discounted resort rooms as part of the Disney Armed Forces Salute. The amount of the discount is based upon the Disney resort price category and varies from 30 to 40 percent off of the full regular rates (30% off the Disney's Paradise Pier Hotel, 35% off Disneyland Hotel & 40% off Disney's Grand Californian Hotel). Starting in 2018 Disney is not offering a set percentage off of each hotel, discount amounts vary but are "up to" the previously stated percentages, though sometimes lower.

Disney has several different "price seasons" through the year, as well as two different prices during most weeks no matter the price season. Friday and Saturday nights are often priced at a higher rate than the rest of the week. Because of this there are numerous different prices for each room based on the date and day of the week. The price for your room even with the military discount can vary greatly based upon the time of year that you go.

Disneyland has numerous different room types differentiated by resort and view. The resort that you stay at (Paradise Pier Hotel, Disneyland Hotel, or Grand Californian Hotel and Spa) affects the size of the rooms and the amenities offered by the resort. The room view also affects your price within that resort as rooms with parking lot views are cheaper than the one's looking out on a pool, Downtown Disney, or a theme park.

The combination for the room and ticket offers have allowed many military families to afford a Disney vacation over the years.

You will find much more information about the Salute room discounts in the Disney Armed Forces Salute Chapter.

Other Military Discounts

There are other establishments (resorts, restaurants, and entertainment venues) both on and off Disney property as well as other theme parks in the Anaheim area, which offer military discounts on a full time or occasional basis.

Read all about these in the Other Things to Do at Disneyland chapter.

The Future

As I said above Disney's Armed Forces Salute is a temporary offer. By this I mean that it is renewed on an annual basis and that Disney has not committed to making it a permanent discount.

The Salute has been running almost continuously since January 2009. There was a 3-day break in resort room discounts and a 22-day break in ticket discounts during October 2010 when one offer ended and the next had a rough start.

You might have also noted a trend as you read earlier, that being that Disney has instituted military salutes during downturns in the economy that affect the travel industry. When the travel industry improves there is always the possibility that Disney will discontinue offering the Salutes as they have done so in the past.

The summer of 2016 saw a downturn in attendance, which surely helped in the decision to continue for 2017; and then spring 2017 saw projected attendance so low that Disney World cancelled their ticket blockout dates (dates the tickets could not be used) for the Disney Armed Forces Salute tickets during Spring Break. The 2018 and 2019 Offers have no blockout dates for tickets (though they do for rooms).

Disney has repeatedly stated in recent years their commitment to the military community, so we might have reached the point of no return for Disney as in recent years the economy has seemed to rebound sufficiently for Disney to stop offering the Salutes, but they haven't.

Wrap Up

The take away from this chapter is that now is (always) the time to start planning your Disney vacation. The 2018 Disney Armed Forces Salute currently runs through 19 December 2018, while the follow-on 2019 offer starts on 1 January 2019 and runs through 19 December 2019. There is no way at this time to know if there will be a 2020 Disney Armed Forces Salute, so if you are on the fence about when to go, just do it!

Ready for More?

The biggest expenses while enjoying a Disneyland vacation are your theme park tickets, resort room, and food. In the next few chapters we'll go over in depth all of the military discounts that are available.

2. Disney's Armed Forces Salute

What's This Chapter About?

In this chapter we'll cover all the specifics of Disney's fantastic offer for military members as well as all of the published and unpublished rules.

The Disney Armed Forces Salute allows qualified individuals to purchase steeply discounted Disney theme park tickets and stay in Disney resort rooms at fabulous discount prices. The offer is for both Disneyland in Anaheim, California and Walt Disney World near Orlando, Florida.

Overview

The Disney Armed Forces Salute is a special temporary offer, which runs for a specified time period. I say it is temporary, because it is still a "relatively" new discount (now in its 11th year) and each self-contained Salute offer runs for a specific timeframe. A new and totally separate Salute must be offered by Disney in order for the Salute to "continue" into the next year.

Each year Disney evaluates many factors (most of which have nothing to do with the military offer) prior to deciding if they will renew the discount or not. The timing of this decision is driven by the timing of these other factors throughout the company, such as annual revenue projections.

Each individual Salute offer runs for approximately one year (give or take a few days). In the early years the dates of the offer coincided with Disney's fiscal year (not the federal fiscal year) starting at the beginning of the first Disney workweek of the their fiscal year and ending on the last workday of the year on dates in either September or October each year.

In 2016 Disney decided to switch to offering the Salute on a calendar year basis. In order to do this they extended the FY 2014-2015 Salute that was due to end on 3 October 2015 through just before Christmas. Then in 2016 they offered calendar year based offer. They have offered calendar year offers ever since.

It is very important to note that at press time there are two totally separate and different Disney Armed Forces Salute offers that have been announced.

The 2018 Salute started on 1 January 2018 and runs through 19 December and The 2019 Salute starts on 1 January 2019 and runs through 19 December 2019.

Eligibility

The Armed Forces Salute is offered to the following individuals:

-Current military members:

- Active
- Reserve
- National Guard
- Coast Guard
- USPHS/NOAA Officers

-Retired military members:

- Active
- Reserve
- National Guard
- Coast Guard
- USPHS/NOAA Officers

-100% Service Connected Disabled with the DAVPRM code on their military issued ID.

-Spouses of the above, in place of the member.

Note the Disney Armed Forces Salute benefit is for the member only. While spouses may use their member's benefit, they are not entitled to a benefit of their own. They only use the discounts in place of the member, not in addition to.

-Non-spouse dependents are not eligible.

-Un-remarried Widows are entitled to their departed spouse's discounts.

-Foreign partners/Coalition partners who are stationed at a US base are eligible. They must have a permanent US Military issued ID (CAC card with blue stripe).

In all cases a current valid military issued ID is required for this discount. VA cards, State driver's licenses indicating Veteran Status, and DD-214s are <u>not</u> acceptable.

Blockout Dates

There are dates during which the Armed Forces Salute ticket and room offers cannot be used. Disney refers to these as "blockout dates," not blackout dates as some mistakenly refer to them, they are dates when the discount is blocked from use. These blockout dates coincide with the very busiest times of the year, such as Christmas week, the peak of Spring Break (as determined by Disney attendance forecasts), and sometimes Thanksgiving weekend.

With the new calendar year offers the Christmas blockout is handled by ending the offer prior to the Christmas rush and not starting a potential new offer until after the rush in the beginning of January.

Ticket Discounts and Resort Discounts

The Disney Armed Forces Salute is actually a combination of two different discounts. There is a resort room discount, which is offered and

by Disney. Then there is the ticket discount, which
 ...s, but is controlled by terms negotiated with the military
 ...ale, Welfare, and Recreation (MWR) establishment.

A very important point is that the Walt Disney World and Disneyland Salute offers are totally separate and any discount limits are not cumulative between the two. You may use your full ticket limit at both Disneyland and Walt Disney World.

Tickets

The Disney Armed Forces Salute offers special military tickets. These tickets are for a specified number of days and come in several varieties.

Qualified individuals may purchase up to a maximum number of theme park tickets per offer.

Currently you may buy a total of 6 tickets per eligible military member during the 2018 Armed Forces Salute offer period. And then during the 2019 Armed Forces Salute offer period each military member is eligible for another 6 tickets.

Tickets from one offer are not valid in the other offer!

These tickets are non-refundable once purchased! The tickets are valid for the entire length of the offer. There is no 13-day expiration like the general public Disney tickets. You may use some days on one trip and the rest on another or take days off during a single vacation. Any days left on the tickets will expire at the end of the offer period.

Tickets purchased at military resellers (base ticket offices etc.) and not directly from Disney must be activated prior to first use, in person at Disney by the military member or spouse. *See the Disneyland Tickets chapter for more details.*

There are no adult or children's versions of these tickets, as there are for all other Disney tickets.

Disneyland for Military Families

The Salute tickets are for ages 3 and up. But, no matter what your age, is a huge savings. Under age 3 is free.

Ticket Specifics

There is only one Salute ticket type that is part of the Salute offer for Disneyland, which comes in both 3-day and 4-day versions.

- The Theme Park Hopper Option, which allows you to visit both theme parks on the same day.

Disneyland Armed Forces Salute Price 2018 (1 January 2018 through 19 December 2018)

- Three-Day Park Hopper Ticket for $168.00
- Four-Day Park Hopper Ticket for $188.00

The Ticket Blockout dates for the 2019 Salute are:

- 23 March – 8 April 2018

Disneyland Armed Forces Salute Price 2019 (1 January 2019 through 19 December 2019)

- Three-Day Park Hopper Ticket for $178.00
- Four-Day Park Hopper Ticket for $198.00

The Ticket Blockout dates for the 2019 Salute are:

- 14-22 April 2019

These tickets can be purchased at your local Base Ticket Office, Disney Theme Park ticket booths, or Disneyland Resort front desks (for registered guests).

be upgraded to 4-Day tickets after arrival for the price difference.

The Armed Forces Salute tickets may be upgraded to any type of annual pass for the price difference between the Salute ticket and the full price pass. Tickets may be upgrades at the Disneyland Ticket or Guest Relations windows.

Ticket Activation

If you buy your Disney's Armed Forces Salute tickets from a base ticket office you will need to activate your tickets before they can be used for park entry. This must be done in person at a Disney location by the military member or by the spouse in place of the member with all of those you are activating tickets for present. Adults must have a photo ID (driver's license for non-military).

The tickets may be activated at all theme park ticket windows, Guest Relations windows, and entry turnstiles.

Once your tickets are activated there is no need for the party to stay together. You may visit the park at different times, visit entirely different parks, and even use the tickets on entirely different days.

Resort Rooms

The Disney Armed Forces Salute offers Disney resort rooms at both Disneyland and Walt Disney World at a great discount.

Qualified individuals may book up to a maximum of two rooms at a time at Disneyland and three rooms at a time at Disney World during the Disney Armed Forces Salute offer period. This discount may be used as many times as you'd like during the entire Salute offer period, unlike the Salute ticket discount, there is no limit to the number of times the discount may be used. The only limit is the number used at one time.

There are Blockout dates during which Disney does not offer the Salute room discounts. These are "peak attendance" dates.

The Resorts offering the discount, room types, and number of rooms at these rates are limited at each individual resort. It is not a wide open offer; rather, when the limit is reached on a specific room type at a particular resort on a specific date, no more rooms of that type at that resort on that date will be offered unless someone cancels. In 2018 Disney started offering the discount on a sliding scale. When Disney has the most need to fill rooms the discount will be the highest, as rooms fill the discount will be reduced until at some point it will not be offered (by resort, room type, and date). To indicate the uncertainty as to what discount you will receive; I've added the words "up to" for 2018 and 2019. You or your travel agent will have to call to check discounts for your dates.

There are very few discounts allowed on the more expensive rooms, while many more are available on the lower priced rooms. You should reserve as far in advance as possible. You must pay a one-night deposit at the time you reserve your room.

The 2018 & 2019 discount rates are:

- Up to 40% off Disney's Grand Californian Hotel (a Deluxe Resort)
- Up to 35% off the Disneyland Hotel (a Moderate Resort)
- Up to 30% off Disney's Paradise Pier Hotel (a Value Resort)

The Resort Room Blockout dates for the 2017 Salute are:

- 9 - 23 April 2017

The Resort Room Blockout dates for the 2019 Salute are:

- None for 2019

Why are there Blockout Dates?

"Why can't I use my Disney Armed Forces Salute tickets or room discounts at Disney World or Disneyland during Spring Break?"

 This is a common response that I hear when military families first learn that the Disney Salute is not valid on certain days.

Since January 2009 the Disney Armed Forces Salute has always had days that the special military discount tickets could not be used for admission to Disney's theme parks or that military resort discounts were not available.

They are typically the weeklong period, which includes Christmas and New Year's a week or two during Spring Break, and occasionally rooms are blocked for Thanksgiving weekend. In the past.

During each individual Salute offer the blockout dates are slightly different, depending on school schedules.

Disney's main purpose behind the blockout dates is to dissuade you from visiting during those times, as there will already be way too many people in the Disney theme parks!

Disney's military salute blockout dates are during peak attendance periods. During these timeframes Disney often closes their theme parks to arriving guests during the day due to maximum attendance. Only those staying on property are allowed in, others are turned away.

These high attendance days, for lack of better words are simply miserable in the theme parks. There are just way too many people, lines are unbearable, and you'll be unable to accomplish all that you'd like to do.

I think it's really a blessing in disguise that you can't use your Armed Forces Salute tickets during Spring Break or other peak times. It forces you to re-evaluate your vacation schedule and plan to go at another (better) time if possible.

Yes, this may involve taking the kids out of school, along class/homework and make opportunities to tur a learning experience.

PhotoPass Discount

Starting in 2017 Disneyland began offering a military discount on the PhotoPass Collection in conjunction with the Armed Forces Salute, this continues for 2019.

What is PhotoPass? Almost everywhere you go in the Disney theme parks, you'll see Disney PhotoPass Photographers. They are stationed at all of the best, most scenic locations at which you can have your picture taken, for example in front of Sleeping Beauty Castle.

They are also at some of the character meals and at Character Meet and Greets.

Many thrill rides also have automatic cameras to capture your reactions to the most thrilling part of the ride in photo or video form.

The PhotoPass Clooection is a package deal for purchasing these photos.

Taking the photos is a free service, you can decide later if you want to purchase the photos. Just have your PhotoPass card or park ticket scanned to identify who you are and get your picture taken.

You can then review your photos online at the PhotoPass site.

You can purchase the PhotoPass Collection for the discounted price of $49.00 through December 19, 2018 and from January 1, 2019 through December 19, 2019.

The discounted PhotoPass Collection can only be purchased at the Main Street Photo Supply Co. at Disneyland Park and Kingswell Camera Shop

Disney California Adventure Park by Eligible Service Members or their spouses

For more on PhotoPass see the Disneyland Technology Chapter.

Rules, Rules, Rules...

Disney Armed Forces Salute Ticket Rules

What follows is a long list of rules for the Disney Armed Forces Salute some of these are published online by Disney and some are not. Even though Disney does not publish them online, they are actually how this discount is administered.

Armed Forces Salute tickets may not be used after the end date of the Salute offer. The tickets become invalid and will not work for park entrance at midnight on the last day of the offer period. 2018 tickets may not be used in 2019, and 2019 may not be used in 2018.

Armed Forces Salute Tickets lose any dollar value of any unused days when they expire at the end of the offer.

Armed Forces Salute tickets are non-transferable and must be used by the same person at all times. Disney has procedures in place to ensure this.

The member or spouse may purchase additional Armed Forces Salute tickets for whomever they'd like, family or friends.

One of the tickets must be activated for the use of the member or spouse.

Armed Forces Salute tickets are non-refundable. If you buy them on base and later find that you can't use them you will not be allowed to get a refund.

Armed Forces Salute tickets may not have additional days added on. However a 3-day Salute ticket may be upgraded to a 4-day Salute ticket.

Armed Forces Salute tickets may however be upgraded to Disneyland Annual Passes.

Armed Forces Salute tickets are limited to a total of 6 tickets during the 2018 offer and 6 tickets during the totally separate 2019 Salute offer period.

The spouse may buy and use the Armed Forces Salute tickets in place of the member (not in addition to).

Disney has always had an exception to the ticket limit for large families. By "Large Family" Disney means a mom, dad, and their dependent children. This does not include the member's adult children (without military IDs), parents, in-laws, siblings, cousins, friends, friend's kids, etc.

The exception works like this: For immediate families larger than 6, Disney will make an exception to the 6-ticket rule. For example, if a family has six dependent children, Disney will allow all members of the family to purchase Armed Forces Salute tickets; that is for Mom, Dad, and their six kids.

Multiple Salute tickets may be used back to back by the same individual(s), up to the offer limit. This is good for smaller parties that want more than 3 or 4 park days per person.

The member or spouse must activate tickets purchased at military resellers (Base Ticket Offices) in person with all members of their party present at the Disney parks. What this means is that you cannot activate a ticket for someone who isn't with you. If some members of your party will not join you until sometime later in your trip, you may activate tickets for those with you initially, and then when the stragglers arrive you may then activate their tickets, as long as you have not fully used up your ticket.

A picture ID of any type is required for all adults during the activation process. The member or spouse doing the activation needs a valid military ID.

Those on terminal leave must have a current military ID; DEERS and VA Cards do not qualify.

Tickets purchased directly from Disney are activated during the purchase process.

One ticket must be activated for the use of the member or spouse unless they are a Disney pass holder.

Members or spouses who have a Disney Annual Pass may purchase Armed Forces Salute tickets for those accompanying them without obtaining one for themselves. One Salute ticket must remain un-purchased in reserve for the member though.

Once the tickets are activated the party can split up. For example some go to one park and some to another, or even use the tickets on entirely different days through the end of the offer period. The Military ID is checked only upon ticket activation.

Disney Armed Forces Salute Room Discount Rules

The number of rooms allocated for this offer is limited. Minimum length of stay requirements may apply for Friday or Saturday arrivals.

Members or their spouses may book up to a maximum of two rooms at a time at Disneyland using the discount. The member or spouse must occupy one of the rooms. All rooms must be at the same resort and check in on the same day.

Valid Military ID will be required upon check-in for the military member (or spouse).

No group rates or other discounts apply.

Advance reservations required.

Additional per-adult charges apply if there are more than two adults per room.

Members or their spouses may use the Armed Forces Salute room discount as many times as they'd like during the offer period at both Disneyland and Walt Disney World.

There are blockout dates when the discount is not valid. Stays on those nights would be at the full price or another discount rate if available.

Disney charges each night individually at the rate for that day (different rate seasons, Salute blockout dates, etc.) The rate at check in does not carry through the entire stay.

The number of rooms and room types at these rates are limited. Once the set number (not published) of each room type at a specific resort is sold out for a specific date the discount becomes unavailable for that room type at that specific resort on that specific date.

All room types from the basic Standard view, to 2-bedroom DVC suites are eligible for the room discount, based upon availability.

The more expensive rooms are offered in much smaller quantities.

The Armed Forces Salute room discount is what Disney calls a "room only" reservation. The tickets that you will use on your trip are up to you to provide because they expect you to use the separately purchased Salute tickets. You may use any ticket that you are able/eligible to purchase with your room reservation.

The Armed Forces Salute room discount cannot be stacked or combined with any other Disney room discount or special offer, for instance other general public discounts or packages.

Why are there all these rules?

There are so many rules associated with the Disney Armed Forces Salute because of what a fantastic deal it is. The rules are there to keep people from abusing the offer.

Disney makes this generous offer to help military families. The intent of the discount is for the military member to spend time with family and friends at Disney's Resorts and in the parks or for the spouse to be able to do so when the member can't go.

Disney does not intend for members to buy these half off tickets (with their funds or for other's) and give them away to people who are not eligible and will be going without the member or worse yet for the member to sell them for a profit.

Disney – "Armed Forces Salute tickets may be purchased at participating U.S. military sales outlets ONLY by Eligible Service Members or their spouses (but not both), for use by themselves and other family members and friends, as provided herein. **These Tickets may not be otherwise transferred, distributed or resold.** "

Military Disney Tips

- The Disney Armed Forces Salute is the single best discount ever for the military community! It makes a Disney vacation so much more affordable. If you are on he fence about going, I say GO while these discounts are still available.

- Remember the room discounts are unlimited, so you can plan several trips with some non-park days for relaxation.

Wrap Up

Well, that was a lot to take in. But the Disney Armed Forces Salute is the best thing to come along in recent history for military families to save on their Disney vacations! If you can work within the guidelines, you will save significantly!

Ready for More?

In this chapter we learned about the Disney Armed Forces Salute, a wonderful combination of ticket and room discounts offered to the military community by the Walt Disney Company.

In the following chapters we are going to get more in-depth into areas like tickets, rooms, and dining. In each of the following chapters, where applicable, we'll start off with what Disney and others have to offer military families.

3. Disneyland Tickets

What's This Chapter About?

In this chapter we will be discussing different types of Disneyland tickets that are available to you as a military family.

We'll discuss each type, where and how you can get them, and then wrap up with a discussion of how to decide what type would work the best for your situation.

Disney Armed Forces Salute Tickets

In the previous chapter we learned about the Disney Armed Forces Salute tickets. We learned what a great deal they are and also that there are a lot of restrictions on how and when they can be used.

As a quick refresher, these are 3 or 4-day tickets at about half off the regular price. They come with the Park Hopper option. You are limited to a total of 6 tickets per military member during the 2018 Salute offer period, which started on 1 January 2018 and runs through 19 December 2018. Then another 6 tickets per military member during the 2019 Salute offer period, which starts on 1 January 2019 and runs through 19 December 2019.

There are blockout dates for theses tickets:

Ticket blockout dates for the 2018 Salute are:

- 23 March – 8 April 2018

Ticket blockout dates for the 2019 Salute are:

- 14 - 22 April 2019

In some circumstances these Salute tickets are not your best choice, but there is another option for you to consider the regularly military discounted Disneyland tickets.

Regular Military Discounted Disneyland Tickets

These are the same tickets that are available to the general public but at a slight military discount.

These Tickets come in one to five day lengths. The Base Ticket, as it is called, allows entry into one theme park per day for the specified number of days. You may leave and re-enter the same park as many times as you'd like during the same day.

The more days that you purchase, the lower the price per day (when averaged), for days four and five you are paying very little per additional day. This is to entice you to stay longer and spend more on other things, like your room, food, and other purchases.

All multi-day Base Tickets expire 13 days after the first day of use. Or at the end of the year they are purchased in (unless near the end of the year, then they'll expire at the end of the next year).

There are both adult (age 10+) and children's (ages 3-9) versions of these tickets. Under 3 is free.

You have the option to add the Park Hopper Option onto your Base Ticket.

Park Hopper Option: Allows guests to visit both theme parks on the same day. You may enter both theme parks (Disneyland and California

Adventure) as many times as you'd like each day for the number of days on the ticket.

It is not possible to get a military discount on the regular Disneyland tickets directly through Disney at the ticket window.

The MWR system sells the regularly military discounted Disneyland tickets at a slight discount through Base Ticket Offices. The military discount amount is about four to eight percent off of the full price, depending on the length and options that you desire.

Some ticket offices maintain a good variety of Disneyland tickets in stock, while others only keep a few types on hand. Some ticket offices don't keep any in stock. If you desire tickets that they do not carry, they may be able to order exactly what you want.

Be sure to check on purchasing your tickets at least 2 weeks prior to when you want to have them in hand, as it may take a week or so to order them if needed.

Southern California Residents

Those stationed in or who are still Southern California residents should be aware that there are special Southern California Resident tickets and passes which could be a great option for you. These California Resident tickets and passes can be purchased at California Base Ticket Offices for a couple dollars off or directly from Disney (online or in person).

California Resident Ticket Types

- 3-Day 1-Park (ages 3+)
- 3-Day Hopper (ages 3+)

A valid military identification card and proof of Southern California residency (zip codes 21000 – 22999) are required at the time of purchase for each adult.

California Resident Pass Types

- Disney Deluxe Passport (Some Blockout Dates Apply)
- Disney Signature Passport (Some Blockout Dates Apply)
- Disney Signature Plus Passport

If you live close enough to visit often these passes might be right for you. There are no military discounts available though.

Where can I buy my Military Discounted Tickets?

While the general public has the option of purchasing their tickets right from Disney online or via phone while making their resort reservations, the military population has to jump through some hoops to get their discounted ones.

These are the locations at which you may purchase the various types of military discounted tickets.

Disneyland Ticket Booths

Types of tickets available: Disney Armed Forces Salute tickets. Full price tickets.

Your Disneyland Hotel

Registered guests may buy their Salute tickets right at the front desk.

Types of tickets available: Disney Armed Forces Salute.

Your Local Base Ticket Office

Many base ticket offices sell Disney Armed Forces some or all varieties of Disneyland Tickets. They may not stock all varieties, so be sure to check well in advance of the date you would like to have them in hand in case they need to order your tickets.

Base ticket offices' Salute ticket prices can vary from the Disneyland prices, usually by just a couple of dollars based on local fees or credits.

Types of tickets: Disney Armed Forces Salute, Military Discounted Disneyland Tickets.

Note: Most bases require that you to come in person, but there are some ticket offices that have procedures in effect to sell to you over the phone and ship via FedEx. There will be an additional charge for shipping.

I am aware that Camp Pendleton ITT will assist you long distance, but please note that they could change their policies with time. Others may be willing to work with you as well

Using Your Tickets

When you buy your Disney Armed Forces Salute tickets from a military reseller, such as your Base Ticket Office, you will receive thick paper vouchers (called Exchange Vouchers in Disney speak) rather than your actual tickets, although some Bases do still issue plastic Salute tickets. These special tickets need to be activated prior to use. Some bases will even give you an 8.5 x 11" paper with your ticket numbers on it in place of individual vouchers.

Regular Military Discounted Disneyland Tickets do not need to be activated.

Ticket Safety

Before I close this chapter I want to talk a little about ticket safety.

Please, only buy your Disney tickets from Disney or Military Resellers (Base Ticket Offices) this is the only way to know that you are getting what you are paying for.

There are sites (Ebay, Craigs List, etc.) where you can buy cheap(er) Disney tickets, military or otherwise, but I encourage you not to do so. You could find yourself in a very awkward position at the park entry turnstiles, when the allegedly unused (or ticket with 2 days left on it) has actually been totally used up.

Also it is stated expressly that all Disney tickets are non-transferable, meaning that the person who first uses a ticket is the only person who can use it on subsequent entrances. Disney has measures in place to ensure this.

At Disneyland multi-day ticket holders will have a photo taken for comparison on return visits.

Physical Ticket Security

What If Your Disney Tickets Were Lost or Stolen?

I ask because this has happened to a military families.

One group had arrived in Orlando for their long awaited vacation and stopped at a local grocery store for some supplies. While in the store, their vehicle was broken into and their luggage was stolen along with their WDW tickets, which were inside the luggage.

What an awful situation!

They were a large multi-military member party using an assortment of military discounted ticket types purchased at different bases. Some of

their tickets they were able to have replaced
ITT/ITR kept good records), but others could
buy replacements.

In another recent instance a family stationed in
for a Disney trip and realized once they were in C٤   ₋ ₗₑᵢₜ
their Armed Forces Salute tickets at home. With a receipt from their Base
ITT and pictures of the ticket ID numbers they could have gotten
replacement tickets from Disney at no cost.

What You Can Do To Protect Yourself

If you are purchasing your Disney tickets (Disneyland or Disney World)
from a Military Reseller you should follow these procedures in case your
tickets are lost or stolen.

- Save your receipt! Put it in your wallet, even if it is months till
  your vacation.
- Take a picture of your receipt
- Take pictures of the barcode/ID numbers of each ticket or
  exchange voucher
- Print one set of photos
- Keep another set on your camera/phone
- Send the pictures to someone else in your party
- Keep the tickets/prints/digital copies all in different locations

When leaving for your vacation

Keep the tickets with you!

Keep the tickets, prints, and digital copies separate. Bring your receipt
too. Don't leave them all together in the car or room! Pack some in
carry-on, some in checked luggage, and some on your person.

Then if your tickets are lost or stolen you can use the pictures/prints and
the receipt to get replacement ones from Disney ticket booths at no cost.

Only One Person Per Ticket

All Disney tickets, no matter what type (military or otherwise) are non-transferable. The person who first uses a ticket for entry is then the only person who can use that ticket.

For example you cannot buy one 3-day ticket and use it to get three people into a Disneyland Park on the same day. Instead, you'd have to buy three 1-day tickets.

Only one "day" on a ticket may be used per calendar day.

For example, you cannot buy a 2-day base (non-hopper) ticket and use it for entrance at a second theme park on a day that you have used it previously at the other park.

What's the right ticket?

So what's the right ticket for you?

That is a question which is highly personal and depends on your party makeup, length of stay, and your desired touring habits. Park hopping vs non-hopping makes a big difference in the price of the Regularly Military Discounted tickets.

Here is some general advice to guide you on how to make your own decision. Be sure that you check prices and compute the total for all combinations of tickets possible to find your lowest price.

Note in the below examples I am using adult prices Regular Military tickets, children's are cheaper. In some circumstances it is cheaper for the kids and adults to use different ticket combinations (when combining different types).

One Theme Park day: the Regular Military Discounted Ticket is the way to go if you do not want to Park Hop. If you do want to hop, go with the 3-day Salute ticket, it is the same price as a 1-day regular hopper and you'll have the option for more days if wanted.

Two to three theme park days: The 3-Day Disney Armed Forces Salute Tickets are the right choice.

Four theme park days: The 4-Day Disney Armed Forces Salute Tickets are the right choice.

Five theme park days and over: This length is where things are most confusing!

You will need to price out all of your options based upon your preferences and decide on the right choice for you.

Compare:

- Back to back use of Disney Armed Forces Salute tickets (up to the offer limit) for all or some in the party.
- A combination of Salute and Regular Military tickets for all members or just some in the party.

All members of smaller parties (two or three) or some members of larger parties can use Disney Armed Forces Salute Tickets back-to-back, either two 3-days (for 5-6 days), one 3-day and a 4-day (for 7 days), or two 4-days (for 8 days).

If your party is large, as many adults as possible should use back to back Salute tickets, then the rest of the party can use the next cheapest option.

Those who can't use back to back Salute tickets should mix a 4-day Salute ticket with a regular ticket to get the desired number of days.

Consider buying non-Hopper regular tickets to mix with your Salute tickets as they are cheaper. You'll have to decide which days of your trip that you do not want to park hop and use the non-Hoppers those days.

If just some in your party will be using regular tickets, any members of the party who are between three and nine years old should use these before adults do, as the child's regular tickets are cheaper than adults.

Military Disney Tips

- Your tickets are a big investment. Protect them by documenting your purchase with some pics on your phone. This quick step could be a lifesaver!
- When purchasing tickets at the Disneyland ticket booths, there are ticket windows on each side of each ticket booth. The queue splits into two lines just prior to reaching the end to funnel people to each side. Choose wisely, sometimes one of the next-door booths will have a window or two serving your booth's line (on that particular side). On my last visit when the line split the line to the right had 3 ticket windows all on our booth and the left line had 5, 3 on our booth and 2 on the next one over.

Wrap-up

Making the decision on just which ticket or ticket combo is right for you can be a daunting task. Hopefully I've given you the information that you'll need to make a great choice.

Ready for More?

Now that we've discussed the military specific items it's time to talk about deciding when is the best time for you to go to Disneyland.

4. When to Go to Disneyland

What's This Chapter About?

In this chapter we'll be discussing the many things to consider when deciding the best time for your military family to visit Disneyland.

Because this book was created exclusively for the military family this chapter presents a lot of information which applies only to the military community.

Other Disneyland Guide Books are designed for the general public and start their discussion of when to go with things like crowds, cost, and weather.

Military families have other things to consider first, like block leave, deployments, PCS moves, and the availability of military discounts before ever getting to the point where the general public starts their Disneyland planning.

So we'll look at each of these areas and then put it all together at the end of the chapter.

Military Considerations

We'll first discuss the military centric items and then move on to the general topics. The two military centric areas we will cover are Military Schedules and Discount Availability.

Military Schedules - Leave

Perhaps the biggest consideration for military families is leave!

First and foremost, when will you be allowed to take leave?

Are you in a situation where you can take leave whenever you'd like? Awesome!

But perhaps you're in a situation where you have to take block leave at the same time with your whole unit on specific dates. Or does a six month or longer deployment dictate when you would be able to go, either prior to, mid deployment break, or after? What about a PCS move into or out of the continental US? Is there a mandatory formal school in your future, which would prevent leave?

Because of these things your timetable may be set for you or be very limited.

If your timeframe is dictated for you, then you will have to deal with all of the following considerations based upon those dates.

On the other hand, if you can go whenever you'd like your next consideration will be to ensure that you go when the Disney Armed Forces Salute discounts are available!

Salute Discount Availability

If you do have the ability to choose when you'll go or are trying to choose between times that you are allowed to take leave, your primary consideration is the availability of the Disney Armed Forces Salute discounts for your potential dates.

There are three things which can affect the availability of the Disney Armed Forces Salute, these are: Blockout Dates, the Salute Changeover Period, and the possibility that the Salute offers will not be continued.

Armed Forces Salute Blockout Dates

These are dates on which the Salute ticket and room discounts are not available for use. They coincide with the very busiest times of the year, which are coincidentally when the majority of US schools happen to be on vacation.

You should avoid the Disney Armed Forces Salute Blockout Dates! This is in order to make use of the huge savings afforded by the Salute discounts and to miss the worst crowds.

Disney blocks these days from use for the Salute discount because they already have way too many people coming at the full rate, so they do not want to encourage any more to come by offering a discount.

Blockout dates for rooms and tickets are often the same, but not always. At times they have been a few days off from each other.

The Blockout Dates for the 2018 Salute are:

Salute Tickets and Resort Rooms

- 23 March – 8 April 2018

The Blockout Dates for the 2018 Salute are:

- Salute Tickets – 14 – 22 April 2019
- Resort Rooms - None

Salute Changeover Periods

New Calendar Year Salutes

In 2016 Disney switched to offering the Salutes on a calendar year basis vesus the old fiscal year Salutes of the past.

With the switch to calendar year offers the old Christmas/New Year's Blockout dates are built into the offer end and beginning dates and create a roughly 2-week long buffer period between the Salute offers.

The 2018 Armed Forces Salute runs through just before Christmas (19 December 2018), while the new 2019 Armed Forces Salute doesn't begin until 1 January.

Just be aware that the 2018 Salute tickets will not be usable starting on 20 December and that any days remaining on them expire. If you'll be going during this timeframe you'll need to use other ticket options and there will be no room discounts.

Salute Termination

The end of each Disney Armed Forces Salute offer could potentially be the end of an era if Disney decides not to continue the program. Planning a trip in a period with no Salute offer would more than double your ticket cost!

It is not known if our community would receive any advance indication that the Salutes would be coming to an end, or if they would just run out with no news of a follow-on. But as of right now we are all set through December 2018!

Ticket Cost

Disney Armed Forces Salute tickets will not work during Blockout Dates or after the offer end date – Any theme park entries during these timeframes will require a close to full price separate ticket for that period or perhaps for the whole trip.

See the Disneyland Tickets chapter on how to decide what the right ticket is.

Disneyland Salute tickets from one offer cannot be used in another totally separate offer.

Planning a trip in a period with no Salute ticket offer could potentially double your ticket cost!

Resort Room Cost

Disney Armed Forces Salute room rate discounts are not available during Blockout dates or after the offer end date – Nightly room charges for these periods will be at full price. You may need to make two or more separate reservations in order to get the Salute rate on nights that it is available. This means multiple deposits of one night's rate.

Cost

You'll pay full price for rooms after 19 December 2018 until the start of the 2019 offer on 1 January. Planning a trip in this period with no Salute offer would increase your Disney resort room cost by 30 to 40 percent!

Room Discount Availability

The Disney Armed Forces Salute room discounts are not an across the board always available discount, rather a percentage of available rooms by resort and room type are made available for the discount. Less total rooms available (because of general public reservations) means less rooms available for the military discount.

To compound this issue the Disney reservations call center has traditionally (incorrectly and against company policy) told military families to go ahead and make a general public reservation for their desired timeframe (prior to a new year's Salute being offered), and that after a new Salute is announced to just call back and have the rate converted.

General public rates cannot be converted to military discount rates! A new reservation must be made and the military discount must be available for that resort/room type. Though the cast member on the phone may imply they are "converting" the rate.

OK, now on to the general public info.

General Public Considerations

We've now reached the part of deciding "When should I plan to go to Disneyland?" where the general public starts their planning.

Keep in mind the military specific areas mentioned above as you continue on with these general considerations. If you can pick your dates great, just press on like you are part of the general public. If you have set dates, read on to see what to expect on your dates.

Next you'll need to consider:

The cost for your room, which will depend on the time of year, the length of your stay, and where you'll stay.

The cost for your tickets depending on the length of your stay.

Crowds, which vary by the time of year.

Weather, which varies by the time of year.

Special Events, which you might want to attend or avoid.

How Much Will Your Room Cost?

Disney Hotels - Keep in mind that Disneyland has different "price seasons" for their hotel rooms throughout the year, as well as two different prices during most weeks no matter the price season. Friday and Saturday nights as well as special or high volume nights (long holiday weekends) are priced at a higher rate.

The price for your room, even with the military discount, can vary greatly based upon the time of year that you go to Disneyland.

There are numerous different room types differentiated by hotel and view. Both your Disneyland Hotel and room view selection affects your room price. Rooms with parking lot views are cheaper than ones looking out on greenery, or water (pool, lake, or river), Theme Parks, or Downtown Disney.

Disneyland's resort rates vary greatly depending on the time of year.

There are typically three different Disneyland price seasons throughout the year. They are Value, Regular, and Peak. These are not 3 blocks of days, rather the rates are used as appropriate numerous times through the year.

The more popular a time period is, the more expensive it is!

Below you'll see when the different price seasons are usually in effect:

- Value – January, February, last 3 weeks of October, first three weeks of November, and the first three weeks of December
- Regular – March, early April, May, June, and last week of August through the first week of October
- Peak – Late April, July, first three weeks of August, and the dates around Thanksgiving, Christmas, and New Year

The prices at non-Disney hotels in the area will also vary during the year so be sure to check on their websites or with their reservations departments.

For much more on deciding which resort or hotel you'd like to stay at see the chapter on Where to Stay at Disneyland. There we take into consideration price, amenities, and extras.

How Much Will Your Tickets Cost?

Next figure out the cost for your tickets. If you are considering different timeframes, are they all at a time when you can use the Disney Armed Forces Salute Tickets? Or will you find yourself having to travel when they are not available? If you must go when the Salute tickets are not available you'll need to use the Regular Military Discounted Disney tickets.

Make sure you do a comparison calculation of how much tickets would cost for each of your timeframes.

Keep in mind, the Salute Tickets do expire, they are 3 or 4-day tickets, there is a limit of six tickets per military member, but they may be used back to back.

Your length of stay and the size of your party can affect your ticket choice.

If your vacation length only includes three or four days in the theme parks, then the Armed Forces Salute tickets are the best, cheapest choice. But if you'd like to spend more than three days in the parks, you'll need to carefully evaluate what is the correct ticket or ticket combo for you.

For much more on deciding which ticket or ticket combo is right for you see the Disneyland Tickets Chapter. There we take into consideration party size, length of stay, price, and ticket extras.

How Crowded Will It Be?

Crowd levels can be a big consideration for your Disneyland vacation. If you have the ability to select when you will visit Disneyland you should plan to avoid the busiest times of the year.

When are the busiest times of the year?

When the kids are out of school!

Holidays

Easter week, Spring Break, Fourth of July, Memorial Day, and Christmas see the very highest crowds (more on this below).

This presents a quandary for parents with kids in school. Should you go during Spring Break, Christmas vacations (the two worst times crowd wise), during the very crowded summer months when it is very busy and also very hot at Disneyland, or pull the kids out of school?

I recommend the latter!

Weekends

Before we dig deeper, a discussion of the Disneyland crowd demographic is needed. Unlike Walt Disney World in Florida, a large percentage of Disneyland's patrons are annual passholders from Southern California, not out of town tourists. Some estimates I've seen say that 80% of Disneyland's business is from passholders or that there are over 1 million Disneyland passholders (Disney does not publish statistics).

This makes the discussion of when is the best time to go more challenging than it is for the Florida resort and the statement above to avoid when school is out is just a starting place.

General Crowd Patterns

Lower Crowds

- Mid to late January
- Early February
- Late April
- Labor Day through the Christmas Season except weekends

Moderate Crowds

- Early May
- Mid August through Labor Day
- Weekdays during December until the Friday before Christmas
- Weekends during the Halloween Season

Higher Crowds

- President's Day Weekend
- Christmas through New Year's Day
- Most of June until annual passes are blocked out late in the month

- During large conventions at the Anaheim Convention Center
- During Disneyland Events: D23 Expo, Dapper Days, Gay Days, and RunDisney Events
- Weekends during the Christmas Season

Highest Crowds

- Easter Week
- Mid March through Mid April
- July Fourth especially if it is in conjunction with a weekend
- Memorial Day Weekend

What Will the Weather Be Like?

Temperature – Southern California and Disneyland generally has year-round nice weather. Most of the year is in the 70s with cool evenings. It gets hotter in the summer, but the humidity is low so it's easier to take.

Rainfall – Rain can be a concern January to March. Disneyland has many open-air attractions and restaurants that can be impacted by the rain.

The last two years the spring was when I was able to go and both years it was rainy during my March and February trips.

Anaheim Monthly Average Temperatures and Rainfall in Inches

	Jan	Feb	Mar	Apr	May	Jun	Jul	Aug	Sep	Oct	Nov	Dec
High Temp	71	71	73	76	78	81	87	89	87	82	76	70
Low Temp	48	48	51	53	57	61	65	65	63	58	52	47
Rainfall	2.87	3.07	1.89	0.79	0.28	0.12	0.04	0.00	0.44	0.71	1.38	2.01

Special Events

Disneyland has many special events throughout the year. Some are big multi-month events, while others are small isolated events.

Here is a list of the big annual events that you might want to attend or avoid due to the crowds they attract.

- D23 Expo, every other year at the end of the summer
- Halloween Time at Disneyland, late summer to fall
- Half Marathon, fall
- Holidays at Disneyland, fall and winter
- Grad Nights, spring

Refurbishments and Construction

Disneyland gets a lot of wear and tear and requires a lot of upkeep. Much of this is done daily after hours while the rest of the world sleeps, but all attractions and areas need to have more extensive work done on a regular basis. This involves taking the attraction, restaurant, or area off-line for refurbishment. During this period the location will be totally closed to the public.

Refurbishments usually occur during January through mid-February.

From time to time more extensive work is planned, whether a total remodel or construction of an entirely new area is required. These projects could be multi-month to well over a yearlong. A current example of big construction is the new Star Wars land that will be opening soon.

All of this is a lot to take in, but now you are armed with the knowledge that you will need to make an informed decision on when to go to Disneyland based on your unique circumstances.

Star Wars

Star Wars: Galaxy's Edge (Star Wars Land) is due to open in the summer of 2019. This is going to have a big effect on attendance levels, so plan your timeframe accordingly.

If Star Wars isn't that big a deal to you, go in the first half of the year. If it is a must do for you, tough it out, avoid right after the grand opening, weekends, and California school breaks.

Planning Your Disney Vacation Timeframe

Key Points for military families

If you can't choose your dates, you'll just need to make the best of it depending on when you can go. Your leave dates might be during a great time to go price and crowd wise, or a bad time…

If you can choose your dates and if possible, consider avoiding the Disney Armed Forces Salute Blockout Dates and the dates between offers. I know that is when the kids are out of school, but the volume of people in the parks will be at the very highest of the year and you'll get no Salute discounts!

Resort Rooms

During blockout dates or between offers your Disney Hotel room will cost up to 30% to 40% more than using the Disney Armed Forces Salute room discounts. The dates that are blocked out have some of the very highest full price rates of the year!

Your rate at check in does not carry through; rather each night is charged at the rate for that day. You can't check in the last day of the Salute and carry the Salute rate forward. So eliminate or minimize your stays on days without the Salute discount.

Park Tickets

Disney Armed Forces Salute tickets are non-functional during blockout dates or between offers. Mixing various types of tickets or leaving unused days on a Salute ticket is costly!

If possible plan to finish your vacation before a blockout period or start it after. If it is necessary to have some of your vacation in a blockout period, try to minimize the number of days. The same goes for the timeframe between offers.

Don't leave days on a Salute ticket unless you plan to return prior to the end of the **current offer**.

Disney tickets for the military is a very complex topic that we've covered elsewhere, please check out the Disneyland Tickets Chapter for an overview of ticket types.

The biggest piece of advice that I could give for those who can choose their dates would be: If you desire a Disney vacation, go at the soonest opportunity! Go now rather than wait a year. Prices are guaranteed to go up and there is always the potential for the huge discounts of the Salutes to end.

Military Disney Tips

- Because California's Disneyland guest population is weighted so heavily towards pass holders, short school breaks including weekends have a much bigger effect on daily attendance, boosting it quite a bit.
- Rainy days are much more difficult at Disneyland than they are at its Florida counterpart. This is because so many attractions and restaurants are outside. If you are going during the rainier times of year, buy cheap travel ponchos and just tough it out.

Wrap up

Deciding the best time to go to Disney is a decision that is very specific to each individual family. There is no one-fits-all right answer, it depends on you, your leave availability, and the things you'd like to do on your vacation.

I hope that I've been able to help guide you in making a great choice for you!

Resources

Anaheim Convention Center: anaheim.net/1871/Calendar-of-Events

Run Disney Official website: rundisney.com

Disneyland Refurbishment Schedule on TouringPlans.com: touringplans.com/disneyland-resort/closures

Ready for More?

Next we'll be taking a look at the many varied options that are available when deciding where to stay at Disneyland.

5. Where to Stay at Disneyland

What's This Chapter About?

In this chapter we'll discuss the different options that are available to you when you are deciding where to stay for your Disneyland vacation. For the Disney hotels we'll discuss price, available discounts, the hotels and rooms themselves, dining options, amenities, features, and locations. We'll also go into other options.

Your options for where to stay during your Disneyland Vacation fall into two categories: on Disneyland property and off Disneyland property.

There are advantages and disadvantages to staying either on or off property and you'll also see that all of the options in each category are not equal, they all have different strengths and weaknesses.

In general, staying on property offers in varying degrees depending on the hotel, both higher convenience and quality, as well as a more immersive experience, but often at a higher price. While many off property locations offer you cheaper prices, they are lacking in convenience, an immersive experience, and at times quality.

The Disney owned resorts offer a list of benefits that are included as part of your stay which are hard to pass up. Your desire to take advantage of some of these benefits may affect your decision. I'll detail these later in the chapter.

Every family is different in their needs and preferences and there is no one overall right or best choice. You should weigh all of the various options and select what you think would be the best resort for your situation.

Staying On Disneyland Property

Staying at a Disney owned hotel comes with many benefits, the most intangible of which is that you will feel like you are at Disney during your entire trip, not just while at the parks. Staying at a Disney owned hotel is an immersive experience and so much more convenient.

Check out this list of amenities that you'll receive when you stay in a Disney hotel:

- Participation in Extra Magic Hour – One-hour early entry prior to the scheduled opening time on designated days to the Disneyland Park or California Adventure. The general public is not allowed in during the Extra Magic Hour so you'll have much less competition for attractions. Disneyland – Tues, Thurs, Sat. California Adventure – Mon, Wed, Fri, Sun.

- Charging of your Disneyland purchases (Merchandise, Dining, etc.) to your room. Note: third party vendors like most restaurants at Downtown Disney are excluded.

- Special Park Entrance – Use of a convenient gateway to California Adventure through the Grand California Hotel and Spa.

- Disney Merchandise delivery to your resort (from the theme parks or Downtown Disney)

- The ability to book Preferred Access Dining Reservations between 60 and 2 days prior to check in.

Now let's take a look at the Disneyland resorts and what they have to offer.

Disneyland Owned Hotels

The Disney look. Walt Disney was a stickler for details, and theming at the Disneyland Hotels runs from the most grand, down to the smallest detail.

When strolling around the Disneyland Hotels, be sure to soak up the atmosphere. The look, feel, and music/sounds all reflect the theme of the individual hotel. For example, look around your hotel room, do you see any hidden Mickeys?

What's a Hidden Mickey? It is the traditional shape of the Mickey Mouse icon (three circles, one head and two ears) hidden in plain sight by Disney's Imagineers for you to discover.

You'll find the above type of detail and more in most places around Disneyland if you take the time to look.

There are three on property Disneyland hotels, the Grand Californian Hotel, the Disneyland Hotel, and the Paradise Pier Hotel.

Disneyland does not classify their hotels like Walt Disney Wsorld does, i.e. Value, Moderate, and Deluxe as the distinctions that set the Florida Resorts apart are more blurred here in California. From cheapest to most expensive is a good way to rank the hotels, which not surprisingly corresponds to their ease of commute to the theme parks and/or proximity to Downtown Disney. They are:

- Paradise Pier Hotel, the cheaper and least convenient option
- Disneyland Hotel, the middle of the road
- Grand Californian Hotel, the closest to the action and most expensive

Disneyland Hotels Overview

First let's look at what the three hotels have in common:

- All Disneyland Hotels are within walking distance of the theme parks.
- Room entrances off of interior hallways
- Concierge/Club level floors/sections
- 1 to 3 bedroom Suites
- Standard rooms sleep up to 5
- On site dining
- Room service
- Luggage service
- Fitness Facilities
- $20 per day self parking/$30 for valet (DVC members free)
- In room safe
- Mini fridge
- Coffee maker
- Free WiFi
- Cribs
- Meeting/convention facilities

Below you will see an overview of the three hotels and what sets each of them apart:

Paradise Pier Hotel – The Paradise Pier is the least expensive option when selecting a Disneyland hotel. Here you'll find:

- Medium sized standard rooms (350-400 Sq. ft.)
- Least convenient to the parks
- Across the street from the main Disneyland area
- Single tower hotel with views of California Adventure on one side and parking lots on the other
- Third floor rooftop pool with slide
- Fitness Center
- Conference rooms
- Business Center

- Game room
- Two Lounge/Bars

Disneyland Hotel – The middle of the road price wise. Here you'll find:

- Biggest sized standard rooms (425-475 Sq. ft.)
- Middle convenience to the parks
- Adjacent to Downtown Disney and its Monorail Station
- Three hotel towers surrounding a central pool, dining, shopping area
- Elaborate pools with waterslides
- Kids pool with slide
- Fitness Center
- Conference rooms
- Game room
- Two Lounge/Bars
- Happiest Hotel On Earth Tour, a walk through the hotel's history

Grand Californian Hotel – The most expensive Disneyland Hotel

- Medium sized standard rooms (356-380 Sq. ft.)
- Most convenient to the parks
- Adjacent to Downtown Disney and California Adventure
- Large winding hotel, six floors with room views of Disney California Adventure and Downtown Disney
- Lap Pool
- Mickey Shaped Pool
- Kids Pool with slide
- On site Spa
- Fitness Center
- Conference rooms
- Game room

- 2 Lounge/Bars
- Onsite Child Care Center
- Disney Vacation Club Suites

Disney Vacation Club – The Disney vacation Club is Disney's timeshare program. In California the DVC location is the Grand Californian Hotel.

The DVC portion of the resort offers studio, 1, 2, and 3-bedroom condo type suites with kitchen facilities. These rooms are some of the most expensive rooms on property, but could be an option for big parties. You may pay by the night just as you would for any other Disneyland hotel room, or rent points to use for your stay from a DVC owner through a third party company.

A small number of DVC rooms may at times be available for the Disney Armed Forces Salute room discount.

Disney Room Types

As you read through the following resort descriptions you will see many different room views and room types. Some are self-explanatory, but others need a little explaining.

Here are some basic definitions:

Standard View – This view is of a road, parking lot, roof, or otherwise unappealing view. They are the least expensive category.
Woods-Courtyard View – Just what the name implies
Deluxe Partial View – Partial views of a theme park or Downtown Disney
Deluxe View – Pool
Premium View – Pool or theme park
Downtown Disney View – Views of the entertainment district

Adjoining vs. Connecting – In Disney speak, adjoining rooms means that the rooms are nearby each other, while connecting rooms have a physical door connecting the two rooms. Be sure to ask for what you need.

Club Level includes access to a concierge lounge offering snacks of varying options throughout the day. Breakfast is often offered and adult beverages are on hand too.

For room capacity Disneyland uses "Sleeps up to X Adults" – For example "Sleeps up to 4 adults" is the way Disneyland lists the maximum adult capacity of their rooms. Children may use excess bed capacity. So in practice a room that sleeps up to 4 adults and has 2 Queen Beds and a Day Bed can sleep up to five people as long as only four of them are adults. If there are only 2 adults there can be 3 kids. If you have 5 adults you need a room that sleeps up to 5 Adults.

You will see under each room type several configurations of beds. Some sleep less than the maximum adults listed for that room type. For example: if a room type says it sleeps up to 5, but one of the configurations listed is 2 Queen Beds, then that particular room only sleeps 4, 1 King sleeps just 2, etc.

Disney classifies those who are 18 years old or older as adults. Kids under 18 are free.

Disney Room Pricing

All Disney prices listed under each individual Resort in this chapter are 2019 prices with tax added and rounded to the nearest dollar (prices subject to change by Disney).

These prices are before any discounts, military or otherwise. The highest prices are for Christmas week and the lowest prices are for the second week of January following Christmas pricing, the rest of the year varies in-between.

There are typically three different Disneyland price seasons throughout the year. They are Value, Regular, and Peak. These are not 3 blocks of days, rather the rates are used as appropriate numerous times through the year.

The more popular a time period is, the more expensive it is!

Below you'll see when the different price seasons are usually in effect:

- Value – January, February, last 3 weeks of October, first three weeks of November, and the first three weeks of December
- Regular – March, early April, May, June, and last week of August through the first week of October
- Peak – Late April, July, first three weeks of August, and the dates around Thanksgiving, Christmas, and New Year

Another consideration is that of the Hotel Price Category. Disney's Grand Californian Hotel is, the most expensive hotel at the Disneyland Resort. It's rates start at $568 per night and escalate from there. The Disneyland Hotel is the mid-price offering, starting at $460 per night and finally the lowest price Paradise Pier Hotel starts at $345 per night. Again, this is before the up to 40, 35, and 30 percent Disney Armed Forces Salute discounts respectively that are available for 2018 & 2019.

Disney Hotel Dining

You will find various dining options at the Disneyland Hotels, everything from counter service to buffets or fine dining. All Disneyland Hotels have Room Service.

In this chapter look for these keys to the rough cost of restaurants and meals they offer:

- $ = Less than $15 per adult
- $$ = $15 - $30 per adult
- $$$ = $30 - $60 per adult

- $$$$ = $60 plus
- B = Breakfast
- L = Lunch
- D = Dinner
- S = Snack

General Information

Official check in time at the Disneyland Hotels is 3 pm and check out is 11 am.

However you may check in at your hotel at any time during the day, but if you arrive early your room may not be ready. In this case the bellhops will store your luggage and deliver it to your room later, after you call for it. The front desk will get your cell phone number and you'll receive an automated text when your room is ready.

There is Free Wi-Fi throughout Disneyland's Hotels, but they have not yet extended this throughout the theme parks. There are some areas in the parks where you can get a signal and in Downtown Disney Starbucks offers free Wi-Fi.

Wheelchair accessible rooms are available.

All rooms have a mini fridge, flat panel TV, in room safe (safe deposit boxes at Paradise Pier), iron, coffee maker, hairdryer, and ironing board.

Disneyland Hotels have recreation options such as, outdoor movies and organized pool activities for the kids to name a couple.

All the Disneyland Hotels have a merchandise location where you can purchase Disneyland souvenirs, food, beverages, wine, beer, liquor, OTC medicines, and baby necessities.

Unlike the Walt Disney World Resort in Florida, every part of the Disneyland Resort is within walking distance from the three Hotels. There is no fleet of buses or watercraft to move guests around like

Florida vacationers are used to. The single Disneyland monorail line runs between Downtown Disney and Tomorrowland in the Disneyland Park. A valid park ticket is required to ride the monorail.

The Disneyland Hotels

And now what you've been waiting for, here are the three Disneyland Hotel's full descriptions.

The Paradise Pier Hotel

Paradise Pier room rates are eligible for up to 30% Disney Armed Forces Salute discount based upon availability and Blockout Dates.

Description

The overall theme of the Paradise Pier is a beachy, boardwalk feel. Rooms are decorated with sand and surf themed furnishings. There are even beach ball pillows on the bed!

This hotel is the lowest priced one on property, which is why it qualifies for the lowest Disney Armed Forces Salute room discount percentage.

At 360 to 400 square feet the Paradise Pier rooms are average size for on property, comparable to the Grand Californian and smaller than the Disneyland Hotel.

The Paradise Pier Hotel has 481 regular rooms and 29 suites.

The hotel is separated from the main Disneyland Resort area by Disneyland Drive so you'll feel just a little removed from the action.

Dining

There are two dining locations at the Paradise Pier, the PCH Grill and the Surfside Lounge.

PCH Grill (BD $$) - Features American cuisine with California/South Western flair. Start your day with the Surf's Up! Breakfast with Mickey and Friends character breakfast buffet. Breakfast items are standard such as eggs, omelets, meats, frittatas, and Mickey waffles. For dinner enjoy the Beachside Bonfire Dinner Buffet where you can have cheeseburger sliders, hot dogs, mini tacos, ribs, and other picnic/bonfire staples.

Surfside Lounge (BLD $) – Enjoy a cocktail or light meal in this lounge off the lobby. Breakfast pastries, flatbreads, burritos, coffee, burgers, sandwiches, and salads.

The Sand Bar (S $) – This poolside location is open seasonally and offers hotdogs, sandwiches, snacks, and specialty drinks.

Features

Pool – The Paradise Pool is a third floor rooftop pool.

Kiddy Pool – The little ones can splash and play.

Hot Tub – co-located with the pools.

A Magical Night at the Movies – Watch complimentary screenings of Disney films on select nights on the rooftop pool deck.

Arcade – Flounder's Fun n' Games Arcade, play video and pinball games at this arcade in the Cinema Hall building, near the food court.

Fitness Center - Work out while on vacation at the Mickey's Beach Fitness Center, a workout facility featuring high tech equipment.

Guest Laundry - Enjoy 24-hour self-service laundry rooms, as well as dry cleaning and valet laundry services.

Meeting and Banquet Facilities

In room Dining

Available at the Grand Californian Hotel:

Child Care – At Pinocchio's workshop kids 5 to 12 years of age can enjoy a night of activities and games for an extra fee.

Mandara Spa - Nurture your mind and body at this exotic retreat where the time-honored traditions of the East meet the science of the West.

Location

The Paradise Pier Hotel is located on the west side of Disneyland property, on the far side of Disneyland Drive from the rest of the resort.

Price

Standard View Room: $345 - $525

Premium View Room: $408 - $651

Standard View Club Level: $487 - $744

Premium View Club Level: $537 - $782

1-Bedroom Suites: - Call for price and availability

2-Bedroom Suites: - Call for price and availability

Signature Suites: Call for price and availability

Room Notes

Standard View Room - Sleeps up to 4 adults with 2 Queen Beds and a Day Bed, or 1 King Bed and 1 Queen Sleeper Sofa. Views are of Disneyland Drive or Parking lots.

Premium View Room - Sleeps 4 adults with 2 Queen Beds and a Day Bed or 1 King Bed and 1 Queen Sleeper Sofa. California Adventure View

Standard View Club Level - Sleeps up to 5 adults with 2 Queen Beds and a Day Bed, or 1 King Bed and 1 Queen Sleeper Sofa. Views are of Parking lots.

Premium View Club Level - Sleeps 5 adults with 2 Queen Beds and a Day Bed or 1 King Bed and 1 Queen Sleeper Sofa. California Adventure View

1-Bedroom Suites - Sleeps up to 7 adults with 2 Queen Beds and 1 Queen-Size Sleeper Sofa and 1 Twin-Size Sleeper Chair or 2 Queen Beds and 1 Queen-Size Sleeper Sofa. Views of Theme Park, Disneyland Drive or Parking Area.

2-Bedroom Suites - Sleeps up to 11 adults with 2 Queen Beds, 1 King Bed, and 2 Queen-Size Sleeper Sofas or 2 Queen Beds, 1 King Bed, and 1 Queen-Size Sleeper Sofa or 2 Queen Beds, 1 King Bed, 2 Queen-Size Sleeper Sofas, and 1 Twin-Size Sleeper Chair. Views of Theme Park or Parking Area.

Signature Suites - Themed Suites are offered and are named: Dana Point, Newport, Huntington, Laguna, Malibu. These suites can sleep up to 13 adults in the following configurations:

- 1 Queen-Size Sleeper Sofa and 1 King Bed or
- 1 King Bed, 1 Queen-Size Sleeper Sofa, and 2 Queen Beds
- 1 King Bed, 1 Queen-Size Sleeper Sofa, 4 Queen Beds, and 1 Day Bed
- 2 King Beds, 2 Queen-Size Sleeper Sofas, and 1 Double-Size Sleeper Sofa
- 1 King Bed, 1 Queen-Size Sleeper Sofa, 2 Queen Beds, and 1 Day Bed
- 1 King Bed, 2 Queen Beds, 1 Queen-Size Sleeper Sofa, 1 Double-Size Sleeper Sofa, and 1 Day Bed
- 1 King Bed, 1 Queen-Size Sleeper Sofa, and 1 Double-Size Sleeper Sofa.

Disneyland Hotel

The Disneyland Hotel room rates are eligible for up to 35% Disney Armed Forces Salute discount based upon availability and Blockout Dates.

Description

The theme of the Disneyland Hotel is ultra modern. Rooms at the Disneyland Hotel are both sophisticated and whimsical, paying loving tribute to the classic years of Disneyland Park.

At 425 to 475 square feet the Disneyland Hotel rooms that range from comparable to larger than those at the Paradise Pier and larger than the Grand Californian Hotel.

The Disneyland Hotel has 990 regular rooms and 60 suites.

The hotel is located adjacent to Downtown Disney. You can walk through Downtown Disney to both Disneyland Park and Disney's California Adventure Park, or catch the monorail in Downtown Disney to Tomorrowland in The Disneyland Park.

Dining

Steakhouse 55 – B $$ D $$$ - Table Service - Premium prime steaks, chops and seafood in an elegant Old Hollywood atmosphere. Breakfast items are standard, eggs, omelets, pancakes, waffles, steak and eggs, etc. For dinner enjoy multiple varieties of steaks plus chicken, lobster, salmon, and lamb. Entrées start at $40 each, salads and sides are extra.

Tangaroa Terrace – BLD $ - Quick Service – For Breakfast platters, wraps, waffles. Lunch and dinner is burgers, salads, and sandwiches.

Goofy's Kitchen – BD $$$ - Character Dining, Buffet Service - At breakfast, 5 food stations offer you choices galore from made-to-order omelets to chicken enchiladas. Munch on Mickey Mouse waffles and pancakes, French toast, sausage, bacon, eggs Benedict, frittata, glazed ham, smoked salmon, pastries, fresh fruit as well as heartier fare like chicken and fried rice. In the evening offerings include meats from a carving station, fresh catch of the day, seasonal vegetables, chilled tossed salads, Pluto's hot dogs, assorted pizzas, Goofyroni and cheese, and hot desserts like bread pudding, fruit cobbler and Bananas Foster crepes.

The Coffee House – BS $ - Pastries, salads and sandwiches.

Trader Sam's Enchanted Tiki Bar – S$ - Specialty Drinks, beer, and wine. Appetizers, burgers, and sandwiches with an island flare.

The Lounge at Steakhouse 55 – S$ - Cocktails, Flatbreads, salads, and bar food.

Features

Two Pools – Both pools have recently been renovated and are fantastic!

E-Ticket Pool - Featuring the Monorail Waterslides, the 2 winding waterslides feature replicas of the original Disneyland Mark 1 Monorail trains. Make a big splash from the approximate 25-foot-high, 180-foot-long Red Monorail slide or enjoy a more relaxing splashdown atop the 13-foot-high, 80-foot-long Yellow Monorail slide.

D-Ticket Pool - The D-Ticket pool is an ideal place for Guests looking to relax or swim laps. A more serene experience, you can lounge the day away in the bubbling Mickey or Minnie Spa whirlpool, or sunbathe from the comfort of a private, poolside cabana for an added fee.

Kiddy Splash Area – The little ones can splash and play.

Hot Tub - co-located with the pools.

A Magical Night at the Movies – Watch a favorite Disney film on select nights under the stars.

Fitness Center - Work out while on vacation at the Goofy About Health Club, a workout facility featuring high tech equipment.

Guest Laundry - Enjoy 24-hour self-service laundry rooms, as well as dry cleaning and valet laundry services.

Meeting and Banquet Facilities

Happiest Hotel on Earth Tour - Discover how the Disneyland Hotel was a part of Walt Disney's dream of the "Happiest Place on Earth" during a one-hour walking tour.

In room Dining

Available at the Grand Californian Hotel:

Child Care – At Pinocchio's workshop kids 5 to 12 years of age can enjoy a night of activities and games for an extra fee.

Mandara Spa - Nurture your mind and body at this exotic retreat where the time-honored traditions of the East meet the science of the West.

Location

The Disneyland Hotel is located to the far west of the north end of the property. It is connected to the main theme park entry area to the east by Downtown Disney. It is actually located on the far side of Disneyland Drive, but Downtown Disney runs over the road and you won't even know you are crossing it.

Price

Standard View: $460 - $642

Deluxe View: $499 - $733

Premium View: $537 - $771

Premium Downtown Disney View: $574 - $783

Standard View Club Level: $733 - $993

Premium View Club Level: $787 - $1095

1-Bedroom Junior Suite: From $850 call for price and availability

1-Bedroom Suites: From $921 call for price and availability

2-Bedroom Junior Suite: From $1075 call for price and availability

2-Bedroom Suites: From $1148 call for price and availability

3-Bedroom Suites: From $1384 call for price and availability

Room notes

Standard View - Views are of Trees or Parking lots. Sleeps up to 5 adults with either:

- 2 Queen Beds and a Day Bed
- 2 Queen beds or 1 King Bed

Deluxe View - Views are of the pool area. Sleeps up to 5 adults with either:

- 2 Queen Beds and a Day Bed
- 2 Queen beds
- 1 King Bed

Premium View - Views are of the pool area. Sleeps up to 5 adults with either:

- 2 Queen Beds and a Day Bed
- 2 Queen beds
- 1 King Bed

Premium Downtown Disney View - Views are of Downtown Disney. Sleeps up to 5 adults with either:

- 2 Queen Beds and a Day Bed
- 2 Queen beds
- 1 King Bed

Standard View Club Level - Views are of the pool area. Sleeps up to 5 adults with either:

- 2 Queen Beds and a Day Bed
- 2 Queen beds
- 1 King Bed

Premium View Club Level - Views are of Downtown Disney. Sleeps up to 5 adults with either:

- 2 Queen Beds and a Day Bed
- 2 Queen beds
- 1 King Bed.

1-Bedroom Junior Suite - Views are of Trees, Parking Lot, Pool, or Downtown Disney. Sleeps up to 4 adults with either:

- 1 King Bed, 1 Day Bed, and 1 Twin Sized Pulldown

1-Bedroom Suites - Views are of Trees, Parking Lot, Pool, or Downtown Disney. Sleeps up to 6 adults with either:

- 2 Queen Beds, 1 King Bed, 1 Queen Sleeper Sofa
- 1 King Bed and 1 Queen Sleeper Sofa

2-Bedroom Junior Suite - View is of the Parking Lot. Sleeps up to 8 adults with either:

- 1 King Bed, 2 Queen Beds, 1 Day Bed, and 1 Twin Sized Pulldown

2-Bedroom Suites - Views are of Trees, Parking Lot, or Pool. Sleeps up to 10 adults with either:

- 4 Queen Beds and 1 Queen Sleeper Sofa
- 2 Queen Beds, 1 King Bed, 1 Queen Sleeper Sofa and 1 Bunk Sized Pull-Down Bed

3-Bedroom Suites - Views are of Trees, Parking Lot, or Pool. Sleeps up to 12 adults with either:

- 4 Queen Beds, 1 King Bed, 1 Queen Sleeper Sofa, and 1 Day Bed
- 2 King Beds, 2 Queen Beds, 1 Queen Sleeper Sofa and 1 Day Bed
- 6 Queen Beds and 1 Queen Sleeper Sofa

Signature Suites – Themed Suites: Adventureland, Ambassador, Big Thunder, Blue Sky, Fairytale, Mickey Mouse Penthouse, Pirates of the Caribbean Suite. Sleeps up to 6 Adults with either:

- 1 King Bed and 1 Queen-Size Sleeper Sofa and 1 Queen Bed
- 1 Double Bed and 1 King Bed and 1 Queen-Size Sleeper Sofa
- 2 Twin Beds and 1 King Bed and 1 Queen-Size Sleeper Sofa
- 2 King Beds and 1 Day Bed
- 1 King Bed
- 1 Queen Bed
- 2 King Beds and 1 Queen-Size Sleeper Sofa

Grand Californian Hotel

The Grand Californian room rates are eligible for up to 40% Disney Armed Forces Salute discount based upon availability and Blockout Dates.

Description

The Grand Californian Hotel and Spa is the premier Disneyland hotel and you will pay a premium price here. This hotel is for those who really want to splurge on their accommodations. The look and feel of the Grand Californian is that of a mountain lodge.

This sprawling resort is the closest to the theme parks and has a private entrance to Disney's California Adventure.

At 356 to 380 square feet the Grand Californian rooms are average size for on property, comparable to the Paradise Pier and smaller than the Disneyland Hotel.

The Grand Californian has 745 regular rooms and 50+ suites. Many of the two bedroom suites can be split into one-bedroom suites.

The Grand California Hotel and Spa is a joint DVC property. It is both a Disneyland Hotel and a Disney Vacation Club property.

Dining

Napa Rose – D$$$ - Table Service - Upscale Seasonal California fare and an extensive wine list in an elegant setting. Offerings include filet mignon, seasonal fish, shrimp, and lamb or pork chops.

Storytellers Café – BLD$$ - Character Dining, Buffet/Table Service – Breakfast features a standard breakfast buffet. During lunch select from an a la carte menu. Dinnertime offers both a buffet or a la carte menu. The a la carte menu features steak, seafood, salads, and pasta.

White Water Snacks – BLD$ - Grab and Go – Standard breakfast items, burgers, pizza, and sandwiches.

In room Dining - Fresh, made-to-order dishes from the comfort of your room.

Napa Rose Lounge – S$ - Enjoy the terrace view or sit by the fireplace, with a refreshing beverage and early evening appetizer or a late-night snack.

Hearthstone Lounge – BS$ - Table Service - Sit by the cozy fireplace of this lodge-style lobby lounge and sip your choice of beverage from the full bar. A lounge menu features snacks like cheese plates, flatbreads and sliders. Coffee and breakfast pastries are served in the morning.

Features

Three Pools – All three pools are close together in the center of the hotel complex.

Fountain Pool - The Fountain Pool provides a relaxing respite amid a serene rural setting.

Redwood Pool - The Redwood Pool includes a 90-foot-long waterslide that curves around the giant stump of a Redwood tree.

Mariposa Pool – The circular quiet pool. Poolside cabanas are available to rent throughout the day.

Note: From January 2017 to spring 2017, the pools and poolside cabanas at Disney's Grand Californian Hotel & Spa will be closed for refurbishment. The pools and waterslides at the Disneyland Hotel and Disney's Paradise Pier Hotel will be available for your enjoyment.

A Magical Night at the Movies – Watch a favorite Disney film on select nights under the stars.

Fitness Center - Work out while on vacation at the Eureka Fitness Center, a workout facility featuring high tech equipment.

Guest Laundry - Enjoy 24-hour self-service laundry rooms, as well as dry cleaning and valet laundry services.

Meeting and Banquet Facilities

The Grand Quest – Search for clues to discover answers in this scavenger hunt through the Grand Californian.

Child Care – At Pinocchio's workshop kids 5 to 12 years of age can enjoy a night of activities and games for an extra fee.

Mandara Spa - Nurture your mind and body at this exotic retreat where the time-honored traditions of the East meet the science of the West.

In room Dining

Location

The Grand Californian is located on the west side of the main Disneyland area. Downtown Disney borders the hotel to the north, California Adventure to the east and south, and Disneyland Drive to the west.

Price

Standard View: $567- $1021

Woods-Courtyard View: $610 - $1086

Deluxe Partial View: $650 - $1151

Downtown Disney View: $680 - $1227

Premium View: $693 - $1276

Standard View Club Level: $986 - $1725

Premium View Club Level: $1087 - $1839

1-Bedroom Suites: From $1327 call for price and availability

2-Bedroom Suites: Call for price and availability

3-Bedroom Suites: From $1993 call for price and availability

Signature Suites: Call for price and availability

Room Notes

Standard View - Views are of Disneyland Drive, rooftops, or Parking lots. Sleeps up to 5 adults with either:

- 1 King Bed and 1 Queen Sleeper Sofa
- 1 Queen Bed, 1 Bunk Bed, and 1 Trundle Bed
- 2 Queen Beds or 2 Queen Beds and 1 Day Bed

Woods-Courtyard View - Views are of a courtyard. Sleeps up to 5 adults with either:

- 1 Queen Bed, 1 Bunk Bed, and 1 Trundle Bed
- 1 King Bed and 1 Queen Sleeper Sofa
- 2 Queen Beds or 2 Queen Beds and 1 Day Bed.

Deluxe Partial View - Views are partial views of California Adventure or Downtown Disney. Sleeps up to 4 adults with either:

- 1 Queen Bed, 1 Bunk Bed, and 1 Trundle Bed
- 2 Queen beds.

Downtown Disney View - Views are of Downtown Disney. Sleeps up to 5 adults with either:

- 1 Queen Bed, 1 Bunk Bed, and 1 Trundle Bed
- 2 Queen beds or 1 King Bed and 1 Queen Sleeper Sofa or Queen Beds
- 2 Queen Beds and 1 Day Bed.

Premium View - Views are of a pool or California Adventure. Sleeps up to 5 adults with either:

- 1 King Bed and 1 Queen Sleeper Sofa
- 2 Queen beds or 1 Queen Bed, 1 Bunk Bed, and 1 Trundle Bed
- 2 Queen Beds and 1 Day Bed.

Standard View Club Level - Views are of a pool or California Adventure. Sleeps up to 4 adults with either:

- 1 King Bed and 1 Queen Sleeper Sofa
- 2 Queen beds
- 1 Queen Bed, 1 Bunk Bed, and 1 Trundle Bed
- 2 Queen Beds and 1Day Bed.

Premium View Club Level - $1444

1-Bedroom Suites - Views are of Trees, California Adventure, Pool, or Downtown Disney. Sleeps up to 6 adults with either:

- 2 Queen Beds, 1 King Bed, 1 Queen Sleeper Sofa
- 2 Queen Beds and 1 Queen Sleeper Sofa

2-Bedroom Suites - Views are of Trees, California Adventure, Pool, or Downtown Disney. Sleeps up to 10 adults with either:

- 4 Queen Beds and 1 Queen Sleeper Sofa
- 2 Queen Beds, 1 King Bed, 1 Queen Sleeper Sofa and 2 Queen Beds.

3-Bedroom Suites - Views are of Trees, California Adventure, Pool, or Downtown Disney. Sleeps up to 12 adults with either:

- 3 Queen Beds, 1 Queen Sleeper Sofa, 1 Trundle Bed, and 1 Day Bed
- 4 Queen Beds, 1 King Bed, 1 Queen Sleeper Sofa
- 2 King Beds 2 Queen Beds and 1 Queen Sleeper Sofa and 1 Day Bed

Signature Suites: Themed Suites: Dana Point, Newport, Huntington, Laguna, Malibu. Sleeps up to 13 Adults with either:

- 1 Queen-Size Sleeper Sofa and 1 King Bed
- 1 King Bed and 1 Queen-Size Sleeper Sofa and 2 Queen Beds
- 1 King Bed and 1 Queen-Size Sleeper Sofa and 4 Queen Beds and 1 Day Bed
- 2 King Beds and 2 Queen-Size Sleeper Sofas and 1 Double-Size Sleeper Sofa
- 1 King Bed and 1 Queen-Size Sleeper Sofa and 2 Queen Beds and 1 Day Bed

- 1 King Bed and 2 Queen Beds and 1 Queen-Size Sleeper Sofa and 1 Double-Size Sleeper Sofa and 1 Day Bed
- 1 King Bed and 1 Queen-Size Sleeper Sofa and 1 Double-Size Sleeper Sofa.

The Disney Vacation Club

The Disney Vacation Club is Disney's take on timeshares. Members buy into a property and use points for stays at DVC properties worldwide.

DVC resorts offer Deluxe accommodations in studio, one, two, and three bedroom suites. These suites can also be rented through the regular Disneyland reservation process and are eligible for the Disney Armed Forces Salute of up to 40% off room discount, though the number available is very limited.

The Villas at Disney's Grand Californian consist of 48 two-bedroom equivalent villas and two Grand Villas.

Disney Resort Wrap Up

That's it for our tour of the Disneyland owned hotels. In the next section of this chapter we'll cover your off property options.

Staying Off Disneyland Property

Because of the compactness of the Disneyland Resort and the fact that it is located right in the middle of Anaheim and it is surrounded and bisected by city streets, staying "off property" doesn't have the transportation issues that staying off property does at Walt Disney

World. In fact at Disneyland, some of the non-Disney hotels are a shorter walk to the main theme park entrances thank the Paradise Pier or Disneyland Hotel are.

Staying off property usually comes with a smaller price tag and may be an appropriate choice for your family. Be sure to research military/government discounts or stays for points through the hotel's websites!

Disneyland Good Neighbor Hotels

The three Disneyland hotels do not have the capacity to house the volume of travelers that come to visit Disneyland on a daily basis.

Because of this, years ago Disneyland created relationships with local hotels which they designated as "Good Neighbor Hotels." You can book packages through Disney that include stays at the Good Neighbor Hotels.

There are 41 Good Neighborhood Hotels in the vicinity of Disneyland. Five of these are across the street, 16 are within a half-mile, and another 13 are within a mile. The rest are over a mile away.

Some of these hotels are national chains and others are one-offs that sprung up around Disneyland. You can check them all out on the Disneyland website.

Be aware that stays at Good Neighbor Hotels booked through Disneyland do not qualify for the Disney Armed Forces Salute room discounts. Also because these are packages, they preclude the use of the highly discounted Disney Armed Forces Salute tickets. Compare your price totals carefully. Reserving direct through the individual hotel for a room only stay and using the Salute tickets, is most likely the best option. Don't forget that you could use loyalty points for the national chains for some or all of your stay!

Off Site Transportation

Some off property hotels may offer their own shuttle to Disneyland and there is also a local shuttle that visits the others. The local shuttle can be purchased at your hotel's front desk for around five dollars per day per person. Inquire about transportation when booking or at your hotel's front desk.

You can also easily walk from most of the hotels located to the east of Disneyland. Walk times are about five to 20 minutes.

Military Disney Tips

- Disneyland offers no equivalent to Disney World's Value Resorts, which offer less frills for a lower cost. Those desiring a lower cost option will need to look off property. There are quite a few options that are within a reasonable walking distance.
- The proximity of Disneyland's hotels makes it easy to head back to the room for a mid-day break to allow the little ones some time to rest and reset for the evening.

Wrap-up

Well, that's it for our look at the options open to you for where to stay on your Disneyland vacation.

Each family's situation, needs, and preferences are different (even on different trips). I hope that I've given you the information that you will need in order to decide what the best choice is for you.

Ready for More?

Next we'll be taking a tour of Disneyland's two theme parks. The next chapter will give you a good overview of and what they each has to offer.

6. Disneyland Resort's Theme Parks

What's This Chapter About?

In this chapter we will be going over the two Disneyland theme parks, you'll get a good overview of each park and what it has to offer.

Disneyland has two different theme parks, the Disneyland Park and Disney's California Adventure.

The two parks vary in size, look, and feel, but both offer attractions (that's Disney speak for rides and shows), entertainment, parades, and nighttime spectaculars. You'll also find many varieties of food at various prices, plus lots of souvenirs for sale.

Attractions

Some of the more intense attractions have height restrictions. If children are shorter than the set limit they cannot experience the attraction. Disney will not bend on these restrictions as they are for safety purposes; in many cases they have to do with the attraction seating and associated restraint capability.

Disneyland, unlike Walt Disney World, also has some attractions with age restrictions, which are for supervision (and safety) purposes.

Attractions with height restrictions will be designated in this chapter like this: *(H33)* the H designates height restriction and the following number designates how many inches tall you must be in order to ride. In this example *(H33)* the number stands for 33 inches tall. Attractions with an age restriction will have it added like this *(H33, 3Yrs)*

At all Disneyland attractions you may "Rider Switch." If you have a little one who is too short or who doesn't want to ride the attraction, your family will not have to wait in line twice for each parent to ride while the other stays with the child. Simply tell the attraction cast members that you'd like to Rider Switch. Then after waiting in line, one parent will wait near the boarding area with the child while the other rides. Once the first parent to ride finishes, they will then wait with the child while the other parent rides.

Where appropriate I'll be describing the seating capacity and layout of the attractions in the parks. You will find all types of ride vehicles at Disneyland, from small continuous feed ride systems to huge stadium seating theaters.

Many rides are of the continuous feed variety. This means that the ride vehicles are mounted one after the other on a track and while running continuously follow each other around the track through the ride. The ride is not turned off (except for handicap boarding) and you board and exit the ride from a moving beltway (like at an airport) moving at the same speed as the vehicles.

When I mention seating capacity I'll use terms like theater seating, four across, and 2+. What I mean when I use the + sign which is usually with the number 2 is that two adults can comfortably sit in the vehicle, 3 can squeeze in or mom and dad with 2 smaller kids. You are free to try to fit all four of you in one car or split up into two.

FastPass

Disneyland's FastPass is a free service that allows you to make a reservation to enjoy specific Disneyland Resort attractions with little or no wait.

The following attractions currently offer FASTPASS:

Disneyland Park

- Big Thunder Mountain Railroad
- Buzz Lightyear Astro Blasters
- Haunted Mansion
- Indiana Jones Adventure
- It's a small world
- Matterhorn Bobsleds
- Roger Rabbit's Car Toon Spin
- Space Mountain
- Splash Mountain
- Star Tours: The Adventures Continue
- Fantasmic nighttime show

Disney California Adventure

- Goofy's Sky School
- Grizzly River Run
- Guardians of the Galaxy – Mission: BREKOUT!
- Incredicoaster
- Radiator Springs Racers
- Soarin' Over California
- Toy Story Manina
- World of Color nighttime show

In this book FastPass attractions are designated like this: *(FP)*

For more on the FastPass system see the Disneyland's Technology Chapter.

Max Pass

In 2017 Disneyland launched Disney MaxPass, which allows guests to maximize their experience by enabling the convenience of mobile booking and redemption of Disney FastPass return times. This is done by using the Disneyland Smart Phone App. Disney MaxPass is available as an add-on to your theme park ticket for $10 a day. Disneyland Resort Annual Passholders also have the opportunity to purchase Disney MaxPass on the same daily or a yearly basis ($75).

Guests continue to have the option of Disney FastPass service at no cost by obtaining paper FastPass tickets at attraction FastPass kiosks, just as they have always done.

Single Rider Line

While FastPass and the new MaxPass are great ways to beat the lines, Disneyland also offers single rider lines at quite a few attractions. If you're willing to split up your party, you will be seated in any open seats on the ride, with a shorter wait than the regular standby line.

The below attractions currently offer the 'Single Rider' option. If you can't locate the single rider line, see the Cast Member at the entrance and they will direct you. This is great if you have teenagers who like to ride the same ride over and over again.

Disneyland Park

- Matterhorn Bobsleds
- Splash Mountain
- Indiana Jones Adventure

Disney California Adventure

- Incredicoaster
- Goofy's Sky School
- Grizzly River Run
- Radiator Springs Racers

- Soarin' Over California

Seasonal

You will see some attractions and restaurants marked as "Open seasonally". What this means is that during high attendance times of the year these venues are open to add additional crowd dissipation/dining seating capacity.

Disney Characters

Character meet-and-greets are locations where you and or your child get to interact one-on-one with a Disney character, get an autograph if desired, and pose for a picture(s). Disney PhotoPass photographers are almost always on hand. Some meet and greets are "open air" where people queue up at an outdoor location and take turns interacting with the character while everyone else watches, others are semi-private meet and greets conducted for your family in a room/set.

Check your daily park schedule or Disneyland Resort app for times for the open-air meet and greets. The private meet and greets are held in buildings all day long.

For more on PhotoPass see the Disneyland's Technology Chapter.

Dining

Each park offers - Counter Service (Disney for fast food), grab and go carts, Table Service and some buffet restaurants. At least one restaurant in each park offers a character meal.

The many outdoor food carts are too plentiful and ever changing to list here. You'll find carts selling, popcorn, drinks, adult beverages (only in the California Adventure), ice cream and frozen treats, churros, turkey legs, and fresh fruits & vegetables. These are just some of the constantly evolving offerings from Disneyland Outdoor Foods.

During Character meals, designated Disney characters (different at each location) will circulate through the dining area periodically. They will stop by each table for personal interaction, autographs, and pictures.

Advance Dining Reservations may be made up to 60 days in advance at select restaurants throughout the Disneyland Resort and, due to limited availability, they are highly recommended. Call (714) 781-DINE or (714) 781-3463 for reservations.

For more on reservations see our Disneyland Dining chapter.

In this chapter look for these keys to the rough cost of restaurants and the meals they offer:

- $ = Less than $15 per adult
- $$ = $15 - $30 per adult
- $$$ = $30 - $60 per adult
- B = Breakfast
- L = Lunch
- D = Dinner
- S = Snack

Note: no alcohol is served in the Disneyland Park. At California Adventure adult beverages are widely served in both restaurants and at walk up carts.

Shopping

As you tour Disneyland's theme parks you will find a wide variety of merchandise and souvenir options available to you.

You'll find Disney character and theme park centric items like stuffed characters, clothing, hats, and many other varied items. Some of these will be generic; others will be themed for the land or area they are being sold in, e.g. a Mickey Mouse in a space suit in Tomorrowland.

Package Delivery

A great service that Disneyland offers is Package Delivery. Any item that you purchase in the parks can be delivered to either your Disney Resort or to the park entrance (for pickup on your way out). This way you do not have to lug your purchase around the park all day!

Bag Check... Bag Check...... Bag Check!

All guests entering Downtown Disney and Disney's parks will have to pass through a bag check area prior to entering. All bags, purses, backpacks, camera bags, coolers, etc. must be opened for a visual inspection by Disneyland Security.

Those without bags or cameras without a bag may bypass the bag check and walk right through. Please have all pockets on your bag open prior to reaching the Security Cast Member to speed things up and keep the line moving.

Metal detector checks are now performed just past the bag check area. You'll have to empty your pockets and then pass through the detector.

Bag Check areas are at all entrances to Downtown Disney and the theme park esplanade area.

Strollers, Wheel Chairs, and Scooters

Strollers, wheel chairs, and scooters, are available for rent from Disneyland at the Esplanade between the theme parks. Strollers are located to the far left when facing California Adventure, scooters to the far right.

Strollers Rent for:

- 1 Stroller $15 per day
- 2 individual Strollers $25 per day

Wheelchairs Rent for:

- $32 per day, which includes a $20 refundable deposit if you return the wheelchair to the rental location with receipt

Scooters Rent for:

- $50 per day, which includes a $20 refundable deposit if you return the wheelchair to the rental location with receipt and key

Lockers

Lockers are available for rent on a daily basis in the Esplanade area between the theme parks, to the far left when facing California Adventure. Many find it convenient to stash sweatshirts for later in the evening, purchases, camera bags, or other bulky items for later retrieval.

Current rates are:

- $7 per day for a Standard Locker (Holds 1 Backpack)
- $10 per day for a Large Locker (Holds 2 Backpacks)

- $15 per day for a Jumbo Locker (Holds 3 Backpacks)

Theme Park Hours

The regular hours of operation of Disneyland's theme parks vary depending on the time of year and expected attendance. Below is a general overview, excluding Extra Magic Hours.

Disneyland Park – The hours of operation at Disneyland vary the most opening between 8 am and 10 am and closing anywhere from 6 pm to 2am.

As a general rule, about the same amount of attractions can be accomplished on a short day as can be on a long day. This is because of the much lower crowd levels and associated attraction wait times on short days.

Disney's California Adventure – DCA opens between 8 am and 10 am and closes anywhere from 6 pm to 1am. Typically DCA closes 1 to 2 hours prior to the Disneyland Park.

Extra Magic Hours

Participation in Extra Magic Hours is a benefit available to those staying in a Disneyland Hotel.

Extra Magic Hours, or EMH allow Disney's on property guests the ability to spend more time in specific parks on specific days, than the general public.

EMH allow on property guests to enter the designated theme park one hour earlier than the regular opening time. This early start to your day gives you a big advantage, as you can get in quite a few attractions during that first hour when the specified EMH park is relatively empty.

Magic Mornings

All general public Disneyland multi-day tickets 3 day long or more are entitled to one Magic Morning entry when using that ticket. Magic Mornings are just like Extra Magic Hours, except this early entry is tied to your 3-day plus ticket versus staying at a Disneyland Hotel. **Unfortunately the 3 and 4-day Disney Armed Forces Salute tickets are not part of this program.**

Theme Park Capacity Closures

Each Disneyland theme park and water park has a set maximum capacity. These limits are for safety. During the busiest times of the year these capacities can be reached. Disney has procedures that they will implement by stages as a park nears capacity.

The Disneyland Park is the most likely to experience capacity-based closures because it is the most popular.

As people exit the closed park, bringing the number inside back down, Disney will begin allowing others to enter again.

Disney's Hotel Guests are guaranteed entry during these park capacity closures.

A Note About Weather

Southern California is blessed with great year-round weather. Because of this many attractions and restaurants at the Disneyland theme parks are open air, with no covering to protect them from the elements. During periods when it does rain closures can be expected.

Well, that's it for the basics; now let's start exploring the two Disneyland theme parks. We'll start with the first Disney park ever opened, the Disneyland Park and then continue on to Disney's California Adventure.

Theme Park Arrival

All guests with two exceptions will arrive at the entry area located between Disneyland's two theme parks called the Esplanade.

Disneyland's Hotel guests can easily walk to the Esplanade (there is no motorized transportation).

Those driving to Disneyland will park in either the parking structures or parking lots and then ride a tram or shuttle bus to Downtown Disney or the Esplanade (depending on parking location).

Guests from offsite hotels can walk or take a hotel/local shuttle bus. There is a local shuttle service that costs $5.00 per person per day for unlimited rides. It circulates through all the local hotels about every 20 minutes. For your 5 bucks you can ride back and forth to Disneyland from your hotel all day. Inquire with your hotel if they have their own shuttle or this one stops by.

Prior to entering the Esplanade from the east (local hotels and parking lots) you'll pass through a bag check area with metal detector screenings. When entering from the west (Disneyland Hotels, Parking Structure, and a couple of local hotels), you will have already passed through the Downtown Disney or parking garage security checks.

Ticket and Guest Relations windows are located on each side of the Esplanade for your convenience. You are now just steps away from the park entrances in this entry area. Disneyland is to the north and California Adventure to the south.

The two exceptions to entering through the Esplanade are the rear entrance to California Adventure only for Disney's Hotel guests and those who choose to take the monorail from Downtown Disney directly to Tomorrowland in the Disneyland Park. These both have their own security checks.

Disneyland Park

The Disneyland theme park is the Disneyland Resort's busiest theme park with twice the annual attendance of California Adventure.

Disneyland is divided into different areas or lands as Disney calls them. Each land is themed much as you'd expect based upon its name. The theming includes the architecture, cast member costumes, types of attractions and food, and even the background music.

You'll enter Disneyland at the south end of Main Street USA, one of the themed lands.

At the far (north) end of Main Street is the hub, the central area around which the rest of the lands are arranged. Sleeping Beauty Castle sits on the far side of the hub. Moving clockwise around the hub are the entrances to: Adventureland, New Orleans Square, Critter Country, Frontierland, Fantasyland, Mickey's Toontown, and finally Tomorrowland.

New Orleans Square and Critter Country are accessed through Adventureland or Frontierland and Mickey's Toontown through Fantasyland.

Main Street USA

Main Street U.S.A. is a Disney re-creation of early 20th century small-town America. Here you can grab a treat for breakfast, shop, spend some time with President Lincoln, or ride on antique vehicles.

Attractions

Disneyland Railroad – Ride on a real steam train on an approximately 20-minute journey around the Disneyland Park. Your train returns to Main Street after stops at New Orleans Square, Mickey's Toontown, and Tomorrowland. You may board or exit at any stop. The five trains that run this loop were all built around the turn of the century in the U.S. There are usually three trains running each day. You can board or exit at any stop.

Flag Retreat – Though not an actual attraction it is highly recommended! This awesome event is held daily at 5 p.m. Unlike at Walt Disney World in Florida, a military member or retiree **is not** selected at random daily to participate, only Disneyland cast members conduct the ceremony.

The Disney Gallery – Presents the Disneyland Story featuring Great Moments with Mr. Lincoln – The Disneyland Story takes you on a nostalgic look at Disneyland, with photos, maps, videos, and other memorabilia from its history. Great Moments with Mr. Lincoln is the original Disney Audio-Animatronics show first displayed at the 1964 Worlds Fair in New York.

Audio-animatronics are one of Walt Disney's big innovations, lifelike figures (human or animal) that are animated via hydraulics, pneumatics, and mechanics, with movements timed precisely to an audio track. You'll find these characters in many Disneyland attractions.

Main Street Cinema – A stand up theatre featuring cartoon classics with Mickey, Minnie, and friends.

Dining

Carnation Café – BLD $$ - Table Service - Breakfast includes a full array of favorites, including Mickey Mouse-shaped waffles. For lunch or dinner, you can choose from soups, salads, sandwiches and hearty entrees, plus gourmet coffees, and ice cream for dessert.

Gibson Girl Ice Cream Shop – S $ - Counter Service – Mobile Order - Offers ice cream cones, sundaes, shakes, and floats. Relax in the old-fashioned ice cream parlor.

Jolly Holliday Bakery - BLD $ – Counter Service - Mobile Order - Features fresh pastries, specialty coffees and signature entrees, including sandwiches, salads, soups and quiches.

Market House - BS $ - Counter Service - Enjoy a cup of Starbucks coffee, plus both Starbucks and Disneyland pastries and sandwiches.

Plaza Inn – B $$$, LD $$ - Buffet (B)/Table Service (LD) -Minnie & Friends Character Buffet Breakfast offers all you can eat with omelets cooked to order, as well as other typical breakfast fare. A la carte lunch and dinner entrees feature fried chicken, pot roast, penne pasta, salads, and other home-style dishes. Dessert includes pie, cake, etc.

Refreshment Corner – LD $ - Counter Service – Serves chilidogs and beverages.

Shopping

20th Century Music Company - Pins and lanyards, Disney music on CD

Candy Palace – Freshly made confections a specialty

China Closet – Disney ceramic Gifts

Crystal Arts – Beautifully crafted crystal collectibles

Disney Clothiers, Ltd. – Disney apparel for the entire family.

Disney Showcase – Seasonal merchandise

Disneyana – Disney art and collectibles

Emporium – The largest Gift Shop in Disneyland (pins, toys, apparel, etc.)

Main Street Magic Shop – For the magician in your family

Main Street Photo Supply Co. - Camera, film, developing and PhotoPass

New Century Jewelry - Disney jewelry

Fortuosity Shop - Disney character watches, purses, fashion clothing

Newsstand - Souvenirs

Penny Arcade - Old fashion arcade games

Silhouette Studio - Take home a paper profile silhouette

The Mad Hatter - Hats for all 'Disney' occasions

Adventureland

Adventureland embodies the edge of civilization; here you'll find several different jungle adventures to enjoy.

Attractions

Enchanted Tiki Room – A musical show featuring audio-animatronic birds. You'll enter a theatre for this show, which is put on by 225 talking and singing audio-animatronic tropical birds and flowers.

Indiana Jones Adventure *(FP)(H46)* - When you climb aboard your jungle transport, you're in for an unforgettable ride. You'll cross a rickety bridge, pass pools of flaming lava, and dodge a huge tumbling boulder as Indy helps you try to escape. Ride vehicles seat nine (3 across in 3 rows) and hydraulic actuators to move the vehicle body, simulating a (very) bumpy ride.

Jungle Cruise - Cruise down the rivers of the world: the Amazon, and Congo Rivers. Your campy Boat Captain, who is full of jokes, will lead your 10 minute long expedition. On this ride you will board a boat which will take you on your journey along with about a dozen other people. As the ride moves along you will see lots of vegetation interspersed with audio-animatronic scenes while your Boat Captain spouts a continuous stream of corny jokes. You'll see lions, elephants, gorillas and many other "animals" on your journey.

Tarzan's Tree House - Walk through Tarzan's treetop home. As you follow the stairs, platforms, and bridges that guide you along. As you climb higher, you discover secrets of Tarzan's past, his life with Jane, their animal friends and scientific experiments.

Dining

Bengal Barbeque – LD $ - Counter Service - Mobile Order - Enjoy a variety of kabobs or bacon-wrapped asparagus.

Tiki Juice Bar - S $ - Counter Service - You can get refreshing Dole pineapple juice or Dole Whip (soft serve ice cream) here.

Tropical Imports S $ - Counter Service - offers in-season fresh fruit, soft drinks and bottles of water.

Shopping

Indiana Jones Adventure Outpost - Official Indiana Jones merchandise.

South Seas Trader - Hawaiian shirts, tropical clothing, sunscreen.

New Orleans Square

In New Orleans Square the name and themeing applies mostly to the dining experiences versus the attractions, both of which are housed in different Lands at Walt Disney World.

Attractions

The Haunted Mansion *(FP)* - Ride through this haunted mansion and then the graveyard outside. Once you enter you will be directed into a small room with a group of others and be sealed in. Your Ghost Host will then introduce you to the mansion. *Note at the end of this sequence the lights go out momentarily and there is a medium loud scream heard on the sound track, meanwhile Haunted Mansion aficionados in the group will scream out loud themselves playing along.*

This is the scariest moment of the attraction. Afterwards a door will open and you'll board your Doom Buggy for a tour of the mansion and the graveyard "outside." The doom buggies will accommodate 2+ with small kids. You will see lots of unique visual illusions and audio-animatronic ghouls and ghosts. Beware of hitchhiking ghosts!

Pirates of the Caribbean – This ride is a classic and a must see! Board a boat with about a dozen others to hit the high seas on this 10 minute long trip through pirate locales. You'll see skeletons, pirates and villagers as you float along. The audio-animatronic scenes depict the sacking of a village, you will float through a cannon battle between a pirate ship and seaside fort, then float through the village as pirates loot and plunder. During the voyage you'll be regaled with the Disney pirate anthem, Yo-Ho Yo-Ho a Pirate's Life for Me. Be sure to keep a sharp eye out for Captain Jack Sparrow!

Disneyland Railroad - An approximately 20-minute journey around the Disneyland Park on a real steam train. Your train returns to New Orleans Square after stops at Mickey's Toontown, Tomorrowland, and Main Street USA.

Dining

Blue Bayou Restaurant - LD $$$ - Table Service - Located inside the Pirates of the Caribbean attraction, features appetizers, salads, seafood, chicken & beef dishes as well as its famous Monte Cristo sandwich, all with a New Orleans flair. Healthy selections, Kosher and vegetarian options are available. (Lunch and Dinner).

Café Orleans - LD $$ - Table Service - Offers Cajun-Creole including New Orleans Gumbo. Start with their popular Pommes Frittes, then enjoy a seafood crepe or maybe a Monte Cristo sandwich and finish with some Mickey-shaped beignets. Children's meals are available.

French Market Restaurant - LD $$ - Buffet Service - This is an outdoor, covered patio, located near the train station that features southern-themed dishes, including jambalaya, roasted chicken, salmon, and delicious desserts.

Mint Julep Bar – S $ - Counter Service - Non-alcoholic Mint Juleps, specialty coffee, beignets and ice cream.

Royal Street Veranda – LDS $ - Counter Service - Mobile Order - Features clam chowder in a bread bowl, gumbo and desserts. Specialty coffees are also available.

Shopping

Cristal d'Orlean - Crystal

Port Royal –Nightmare Before Christmas Merchandise

La Mascarade d'Orleans - Pandora Jewelry

LeBat en Rouge – Ladies Clothing

Mlle. Antoinette's Parfumerie - Perfume

Parasol Cart – Custom decorated Parasols

Pieces of Eight – Pirate Themed Items

Portrait Artists - Portraits

Royal Street Sweets - Sweets

Critter Country

Attractions

Davy Crockett's Explorer Canoes - Get ready to paddle. On this real canoe ride, guests do the work as they paddle around Tom Sawyer's Island. Two guides will steer you and help chart your course. This attraction is only open during daylight hours. *(Closed for StarWars Land Construction, will reopen summer 2017).*

The Many Adventures of Winnie the Pooh – Ride in a honey pot and see all of Pooh's adventures. Your 4+ person honey pot will take you on a fun journey through the Hundred Acre Wood where you'll see scenes from the books and movies. Join Pooh and friends in a celebration as the ride ends.

Splash Mountain *–FP)(H40)* – A log flume ride through Brer Rabbit's Laughin' Place. One of Disneyland's favorite thrill rides. Board your eight-person log to float through the scenes from *Song of the South* where you will see Brer Rabbit's adventures while listening to songs from the movie. You'll progressively get higher during this calm portion of the ride. There may be a few small plunges along the way, until you come to the big final drop and splash. You will get wet! Some more than others, the left side is alleged to get less water.

Dining

Harbour Galley - LD $ - Counter Service – Mobile Order - This restaurant on the banks of the Rivers of America offers chowder and soups served in bread bowls, plus entree sized salads, baked potatoes and drinks.

Hungry Bear Restaurant – LD $ - Counter Service – Mobile Order - Offers American type fare, such as chicken sandwiches, cheeseburgers, fries, etc. Kids meals are also available.

Shopping

Briar Patch - Critter Country Plush Character merchandise and more.

Pooh Corner - Winnie the Pooh merchandise

Professor Barnaby Owl's Photographic Art Studio - Photos of your 'Splash Mountain' experience

Frontierland

Frontierland depicts life in America's expanding western frontier, and is home to Big Thunder Mountain.

Attractions

Big Thunder Mountain Railroad *(FP)(H40, 3 Yr)* - Hold on to your hats this runaway mine train is the "Wildest Ride in the Wilderness." You will board a train, complete with locomotive in the front for this rollercoaster ride. This fun outdoor coaster zips through mining town scenery based upon Utah's Brice Canyon with lots of dips and curves. Don't miss, one of our favorites!

Frontierland Shootin' Exposition – Try your best to get a bull's-eye. Shoot up Boot Hill and see what happens in this laser gun-shooting gallery. There is an extra charge for this attraction.

The Golden Horseshoe Stage - Spend some time kicking up your heels with the Laughing Stock Company. In addition to the entertainment at this sit-down theater, you will also find food being served which includes chicken nuggets, fish & chips, chili, ice cream sundaes and soft drinks.

Mark Twain Riverboat – Experience a full-circle cruise tour of the Rivers of America around Tom Sawyer Island upon this steam-powered stern-wheeler paddlewheel boat. It's a relaxing journey that brings the past to life.

Pirates Lair on Tom Sawyer Island – Tom Sawyer Island is a haven for Pirates. Among the enhancements will be a "Dead Man's Grotto" in the island caverns, a "Pirate's Den" on the Castle Rock as well as Buccaneer touches made to Tom & Huck's Treehouse and Smuggler's Cove. Visitors can go in search of buried treasure, but beware; there will be live pirates waiting to take your booty away. *(Closed for StarWars Land Construction, will reopen summer 2017).*

Sailing Ship Columbia – Experience a full-circle cruise tour of the Rivers of America around Tom Sawyer Island aboard the first 3-masted windjammer to be built in the United States in over 100 years. You may also visit below deck to view the galley and living quarters in the ship's museum.

Seating is on a first-come, first-served basis for each show.

Dining

The Golden Horseshoe – LD $ with a show - Grab a bite to eat, sit back and enjoy the show. Chicken nuggets, fish & chips and cold beverages. Grab lunch or dinner before the show!

Rancho del Zocalo Restaurante – LD $ - Buffet Service - Classic Mexican specialties include menu items like burritos, nachos and much more.

River Belle Terrace – LD $ - Buffet Service - Options include BBQ ribs, oven-roasted BBQ chicken or a tasty brisket sandwich. Vegetarian options are available. Kids Meals are also available.

Ship to Shore Marketplace – S$ - Fresh fruit, turkey legs, chimichangas, and frozen beverages.

Stage Door Café – LD $ - Counter Service - Mobile Order - Chicken nuggets, fish & chips, and corn dogs.

Shopping

Bonanza Outfitters - Outdoor clothing for the entire family

Pioneer Mercantile - Souvenirs with a western flare

Westward Ho Trading Company - Disney Pins, pins and more pins

Fantasyland

Fantasyland embodies all things fanciful, here magic abounds. Take a flight with Peter Pan, or a ride with Pinocchio or Snow White.

Attractions

Alice in Wonderland – Climb aboard your "caterpillar" and journey with Alice as she falls down the rabbit hole. Along the way you'll meet up with some of the famous characters from the Lewis Carroll classic, like Tweedle Dee and Tweedle Dum, the Queen of Hearts and the grinning Cheshire Cat. Seating for 4+ in 2 rows.

Casey Jr. Circus Train – This tiny train travels through a hilly area and offers views of Storybook Land.

Dumbo the Flying Elephant - Ride on your favorite elephant, Dumbo. Make him fly up then down as you fly in a circle. Your 2+ person elephant can be controlled to fly up and down on this circular journey.

Fantasy Faire – At the Royal Theatre, Disney Princesses present their stories with the help of Renaissance vaudeville-style storytellers. At the Royal Hall, guests are able to meet three of their favorite Disney Princesses.

Fantasyland Theatre – See the musical story of the Magical Map with Mickey and many other Disney cartoon favorites. Check daily entertainment handouts or your Disneyland app for daily show times.

"It's a Small World" – A Disney classic, audio-animatronic dolls from all over the world plus a few Disney favorites will entertain you during this indoor boat ride. Your boat will seat about a dozen people in 4+ person rows. Each scene you pass through will feature children and animals of the world singing and dancing together in friendship, all to that tune many love to hate or hate to love, *"It's a small world after all."*

King Arthur Carrousel – Features 72 white carrousel horses that were handcrafted over a century ago, with no two being exactly alike. All of the horses move up and down as the carrousel revolves.

Mad Tea Party - Spinning oversized teacups, this 2-minute long ride whizzes round and round while each group of cups also revolves and you can manually spin your own cup. This ride is not for those with weak stomachs! It is 2 minutes longer than it should be for me...

Matterhorn Bobsleds –*(H42)* - A roller coaster ride, which will bring you to an encounter with the Abominable Snowman. You'll twist and turn along the track past icicles and fog until you safely arrive back at the base.

Mister Toad's Wild Ride - Hop in and hold tight on this journey through the library of Toad Hall and the city streets of London. You'll encountering an irate judge and a speeding train along the way. This ride seats 2+.

Peter Pan's Flight – Ride in a pirate ship over the rooftops of London and into Neverland as you follow Peter Pan on his adventures. Board a 2+ person (with small kids) pirate ship for this airborne journey. You'll cruise over all major scenes from the movie until the crocodile catches the Captain.

Pinocchio's Daring Journey – Climb aboard your wooden car and follow Pinocchio through his adventures with Jiminy Cricket as your guide. See the dark side of Pleasure Island, before all ends well when Pinocchio is safely back home with Gepetto and is transformed into a real boy.

Pixey Hollow - Tinker Bell and her fairy friends meet guests at Pixie Hollow.

Sleeping Beauty Castle Walkthrough – Walk through the story of Disney's Sleeping Beauty depicted through original artwork used in the film. Enhanced scenes and visual effects provide a must see timeless classic.

Snow White's Scary Adventures – Ride through and relive the tale of Snow White, complete with Magic Mirror, Wicked Queen, Seven Dwarfs and gallant Prince Charming. Caution, this attraction can be scary to little ones, especially the scenes with the Wicked Queen.

Storybook Land Canal Boats – Board these picturesque boats and journey through a miniature world of many Disney motion picture classics. Boats are scaled down replicas of Dutch, English, and French boats. Each is named after a Disney character.

Dining

Troubadour Tavern - LD $ - Counter Service - Features bratwurst, Stuffed Baked Potatoes, corn on the cob and a selection of frozen desserts.

Red Rose Taverne - LD $ - Counter Service - Mobile Order - Serves flatbreads, cheeseburgers, chicken sandwiches, and salads. This is essentially the same menu as the Village Haus with the addition of poutine (a Canadian dish: fries with gravy on top, in this case with beef as well).

Shopping

Bibbidi Bobbidi Boutique - Salon for girls and boys, with character costumes and more.

Fairy Tale Treasures - Princess costumes

Fantasy Faire Gifts - Film, postcards

Castle Heraldry Shop - Family Crests and Coats of Arms

"It's A Small World" Toy Shop - Toys

Le Petit Chalet Gifts - Character T-shirts, collectibles

Mad Hatter - Mickey Mouse Ears and other Disney hats

Stromboli 's Wagon - Candy and T-Shirts

Mickey's Toontown

Mickey's Toontown is the longtime home of many of your favorite Disney characters. Visit classic Disney characters and enjoy the scenery inspired by Roger Rabbit.

Mickey's Toontown can close early due to fireworks, check the daily schedule

Attractions

Chip n' Dale Treehouse – Children can enter through an opening at the base of the Redwood style tree house and climb a staircase that spirals up through the trunk.

Disneyland Railroad - An approximately 20-minute journey around Disneyland on a real steam train. Your train returns to Mickey's Toontown after stops at Tomorrowland, Main Street USA and New Orleans Square.

Donald's Boat – Walk through Donald's large houseboat, the "Miss Daisy" docked in the lagoon. This is a walk-through experience with fun hands-on activities.

Gadget's Go Coaster – *(H35)* -A children's roller coaster attraction that takes you on an adventure over and around upper Toon Lake.

Goofy's Playhouse – Kids will enjoy Goofy's yard where they can play, climb and slide.

Mickey's House and Meet Mickey – Mickey's house is in the corner of Toontown. Visitors enter Mickey's living room and walk through his house, viewing his personal mementos and show business memorabilia. In the screening room a continuous loop film featuring segments from four of Mickey's early cartoons are shown on a bed sheet serving as a screen.

Meet and Greet: Meet Mickey inside his house. Check the daily schedule for appearance times.

Minnie's House – Minnie's home is right next to Mickey's. Walk through Minnie's house and you'll find lots of pictures of her favorite mouse, Mickey. There is a wishing well in the backyard where an audio response is heard when you speak or drop a coin into it.

Meet and Greet: Meet Minnie in front of her house. Check the daily schedule for appearance times.

Roger Rabbit's Car Toon Spin *(FP)* - Board a Toon taxi and follow Roger and Benny's trail through town while pursued by the Weasels. Take control of the wheel, spinning your way through the Bullina China Shop, the local Power Plant and the Gag Warehouse on a fast paced spinning ride.

Dining

Clarabelle's Frozen Yogurt – S $ - Counter Service - Frozen chocolate and vanilla swirl yogurt is a favorite here! Mickey shaped krispie treats and sundaes also available.

Daisy's Diner – LDS $ - Counter Service - Pizza, salads and desserts.

Pluto's Dog House - LDS $ - Counter Service - Hot dogs and cold beverages.

Shopping

Gag Factory - Toontown Five & Dime - Art & Collectibles; Toys & Plush; Pins & Vinylmation; Camera & Media ; Gifts & Housewares; Apparel & Accessories; Mickey Ears

Tomorrowland

Tomorrowland is a look at what the "Future That Never Was" might look like, as imagined by sci-fi writers from the 1920's and 1930's. Take a spin on the third of the Disneyland's "Mountains", Space Mountain, or help Buzz Lightyear defeat Emperor Zurg.

Attractions

Astro Orbiter - Fly in a circle high above Tomorrowland, make your astro orbiter rise and fall. Another of Disney's circular up and down rides like Dumbo. The ride vehicles look like rockets and seating is 2 per rocket.

Autopia *(FP)(H54 to drive, 1Yr to ride)* - Drive a mini racecar on a two mile-long racetrack through Tomorrowland. These little two-person gas powered cars tool around the track on a guide rail. You can steer side to side and around corners, but the rail keeps you "firmly" in your lane. The combo gas pedal/brake is quite hard to push and is mounted in the center of the floorboard so the adult can operate it while the child attempts to steer. Pre-driving kids will enjoy this, adults will be glad when the left to right jerking and bumping into stopped cars is over!

Buzz Lightyear's Astro Blasters *(FP)* – Shoot your laser to defeat Zurg and score points! Your 2+ person space ship is equipped with two lasers so that you can help Buzz defeat Emperor Zurg. As you move through the various rooms in your space ship you can shoot at the plethora of targets and when you score a hit your points will accumulate on your individual score board. There is also a joystick so that you can spin your space ship from side to side to get a better angle on targets. This is a fun ride for the whole family! See who gets the highest score.

Disneyland Monorail – Travel from Tomorrowland in Disneyland to Downtown Disney Station, which is accessible to the Disneyland Resort Hotels. (When boarding at the Downtown Disney station, guests must disembark in Tomorrowland.)

Disneyland Railroad - An approximately 20-minute journey around the Disneyland on a real steam train. Your train returns to Tomorrowland after stops at, Main Street USA, New Orleans Square, and Mickey's Toontown.

Finding Nemo Submarine Voyage – Via a submarine, you visit the underwater world of Nemo and his friends. Using new technology, the cast of 'Finding Nemo' will swim by your porthole in this fun filled attraction. Listen to the action as Dory, Marlin and friends go in pursuit of Nemo.

Hyperspace Mountain – (FP)(H40) - Ride a high-speed, indoor coaster on a dark track! Seating is two persons side by side. After boarding you'll blast off into space, the coaster runs through an almost totally dark area, you will never know which way it is going to turn or when the next drop is coming. An onboard Star Wars soundtrack and occasional visuals add to the excitement.

Jedi Training: Trials of the Temple - Features Darth Vader, Darth Maul and Seventh Sister from Star Wars Rebels. Kids will train alongside real Jedis to learn the fine art of light saber fighting. Signup is on a first come, first served basis and slots are limited. Signup early near the exit to the Star Wars Launch Bay. This show is fun to watch whether your young Jedi is participating or not. The Stage is next to the Tomorrowland Terrace. Check the nearby sign or daily schedule for times

Star Tours the - Adventure Continues – (FP)(H40) - Get ready for your trip to one of 6 different destinations in this new 3-D version of the classic ride. You'll be traveling to Kashyyyk, Geonosis, Hoth, Naboo, Coruscant or Tatooine, but be careful you don't take an unexpected trip to the Death Star.

Star Wars Launch Bay - Explore both the Light and Dark Sides of The Force, including meeting some of your favorite Star Wars characters, check out props and models from the Star Wars saga and play the latest Star Wars video games.

Dining

Alien Pizza Planet - LD $ – Counter Service - offers pizza, Caesar salad, and pasta. You can eat inside, or "outside" in a covered area.

Galactic Grill– LD $ - Counter Service – Mobile Order - Cheeseburgers, chicken breast sandwiches, tortilla wraps, fries, etc. Jedi Training is presented on the stage during the day.

Shopping

Merchant of Venus - Wigs, jewelry, Stitch merchandise, home decor, and futuristic toys.

Mickey's Star Traders - Souvenirs, clothing, jewelry, film, books, toys, and hats.

Disneyland Park Entertainment

Nighttime Shows

Fireworks – Dreams Come True Fireworks is a tribute to the timeless Disney stories and characters which includes a flyby by Tinker Bell.

Fantasmic *(FP)* - Join Mickey along the Rivers of America in Frontierland and New Orleans Square for this amazing fight against good and evil. Special effects, water projection, fiber optics and lasers make this one of

Disneyland's must see events. *(Closed for Star Wars Land Construction, will reopen summer 2017).*

"Remember Dreams Come True" Fireworks – features Tinker Bell's flight, brilliant fireworks, soaring music, dazzling special effects and an amazing journey through the various lands of Disneyland with archival audio tracks, favorite songs and familiar phrases from some of the park's most popular attractions, past and present.

Parades

The Main Street Electrical Parade – The classic Main Street Electrical Parade, with its thousands of sparkling lights and electronic musical sounds, returns to Main Street USA for a limited time only (Scheduled through 18 June 2017). The Main Street Electrical Parade is a beloved procession of Disney stories brought to life in shimmering colored lights and bouncy, bubbly music. *Alice in Wonderland, Cinderella, Peter Pan, Dumbo, Snow White* and *Pete's Dragon* are featured during the 20-minute spectacle.

Mickey's Soundsational Parade - Features some of the most popular music from Disney movies and some of your favorite characters, including Ariel, Tiana, Peter Pan, Mary Poppins, The Three Caballeros and Aladdin.

Shows & Other Entertainment

At both theme parks you will find a wide variety of entertainment venues and pop-up performances plus what Disney calls "Streetmosphere" characters. These characters are supposed to be residents of the area that you see them in, such as the Mayor of Main Street. These are larger than life characters who both have set performances with scripts (people will gather to watch these) and they will also interact with you on an individual basis when walking around and not performing.

Final thoughts on the Disneyland Park

The Disneyland Park is the crown jewel of Disneyland! The original park with the closest ties to all the beloved Disney films, it has a special place in many people's hearts. This is the busiest of the two parks, the must do park, and one that may take more than a day to explore during your vacation.

The Disneyland Park is in the midst of adding a new Star Wars Land. The 14-acre land will be the largest-ever single-themed land expansion at Disneyland Resort. They still have a long way to go, as the new land is not scheduled to open until 2019.

Disney's California Adventure

Disney's California Adventure (DCA) is the newer of the two Disneyland theme parks. It opened on 8 February 2001, while the Disneyland Park opened on 17 July 1955. DCA received a major makeover plus the addition of the new Cars Land in 2012 and now Paradise Pier has been transformed into Pixar Pier.

California Adventure is a theme park that celebrates California. When you enter you are transported to the land of promise, opportunity and glamour. Disney California Adventure is a journey from the California of yesterday to today and a tribute to this land of dreams.

Arrival

There are two entrances to California Adventure, the Main Entrance from the Esplanade and the Grand Californian Hotel entrance.

The Grand Californian Hotel entrance is an entrance exclusively for those guests staying at Disney's Hotels. It is located towards the rear of the Hotel and enters the park in the Grizzly Peak area near Grizzly River Run.

Guests from all Disney Hotels may follow the signs to the rear of the Grand Californian, where they will go through a security check and then enter the park. The line here is much shorter than you will experience at the front entrance and a valid hotel key is required.

All other, non-Disney Hotel guests will enter at the Main Entrance.

Disney California Adventure has a slightly different physical arrangement than the typical Disney theme park, such as Disneyland, Disney World's Magic Kingdom, or Disney's Animal Kingdom.

You will enter Disney California Adventure at the north end of Buena Vista Street, You'll follow the street south to Carthay Circle where to the left you'll find a street leading to Hollywood Land and to the right one to Grizzly Peak. When you proceed straight across the circle you will find a road that slowly curves to the right around Grizzly Peak on its way to the rear of the park. This walkway leads to the remaining Lands. Along the left side you will find Cars Land, Pacific Warf, and Pixar Pier. Then Paradise Gardens Park will be straight ahead. All the Lands are interconnected off of this main road/walkway as well. "a bug's land" would have preceded Cars Land in the description above, but it closed in Sept 2018 to make way for a Marvel Comics themed Land (opening 2020).

Buena Vista Street

Buena Vista Street is a salute to 1920s and 30s Los Angeles, around the time that Walt Disney arrived in California.

Carthay Circle at the end of the block features a beautiful fountain and a replica of the Carthay Circle Theater, where the premiere of "Snow White and The Seven Dwarfs" was held in 1937.

Buena Vista Street consists mainly of shopping and dining locations, with no real attractions other than the trolley car to Hollywood Land.

Attractions

None

Dining

Mortimer's Market – S $ - Fresh fruit, bottled water and soft drinks.

Clarabelle's Hand-Scooped Ice Cream – S $ - Counter Service – Mobile Order - Serves Dreyer's ice cream, including bars dipped in milk or dark chocolate that you can finish with sprinkles, pop rocks or other fun toppings. Sundaes and other frozen treats are also available.

Fiddler Fifer and Practical Café BLDS $ - Counter Service - Enjoy Starbuck's coffee, espresso, blended beverages, breakfast items and pasteries plus other signature sandwiches, soups and desserts.

Carthay Circle Restaurant LD $$$ - Table Service – The menu focuses on seasonal products and the diverse flavors found in Southern California. For example lunch offerings such as crispy firecracker duck wings or angus flank steak cobb salad. Dinner featuring Colorado rack of lamb or grilled Jamaican jerked kingfish. Menus change seasonally. Reservations are recommended.

Food and drinks are also available in the collocated Carthay Circle Restaurant lounge.

Shopping

Julius Katz & Sons - The Katz family store features gadgets and home decor.

Big Top Toys - Toys, games and plush characters.

Oswald's - Road-trip essentials, including autograph books, hats, bags, antenna toppers, key chains and travel mugs.

Los Feliz Five & Dime - Features collections of clothing and other souvenirs inspired by railways and trolleys as well as character merchandise featuring Mickey and friends in retro styling.

Elias & Co. - The biggest store on Buena Vista Street, Elias and Company pays tribute to the fancy department stores of yesteryear. Clothing and other merchandise featuring retro-style attraction poster art, plus a selection of men's period fedoras and executive-style accessories.

Kingswell Camera Shop – Camera supplies as well as being the place to check out your PhotoPass pictures.

Atwater Ink & Paint – Disney items for the home.

Trolley Treats - Trolley Treats features taffy, caramel apples, dipped strawberries, fudge, toffee and other handmade temptations, plus a working candy kitchen.

Hollywood Land

Hollywood Land is a tribute to Hollywood past and present. Classic architecture sets the tone and transports you to Hollywood's Golden Age.

Attractions

Monsters Inc. Mike & Sulley to the Rescue! - This is a slow moving, dark ride and fun for all ages. Take a ride through Monstropolis, where you will see various scenes from the movie including Harry Hausen's restaurant and watch as Mike and Sulley try to return Boo to her home.

Guardians of the Galaxy - Mission: BREAKOUT! - Deep inside his fortress-like collection, the mysterious Taneleer Tivan (aka The Collector) is displaying his newest acquisitions, the Guardians of the

Galaxy. They are trapped in customized display cases, suspended over a vast abyss. Unbeknownst to their unscrupulous captor, the intrepid Rocket has escaped and is enlisting the Collector's VIP guests for help. Guests board a gantry lift, which launches them into a chaotic and hilarious adventure as they join Rocket in an attempt to break his fellow Guardians out of captivity.

Disney Animation - The Disney Animation attraction offers insight into the world of animation with several exhibits to visit, each offering a unique experience:

- The Animation Courtyard: Features large screens with clips and music from your favorite Disney animated features.
- Animation Academy: Join a Disney artist and learn the secrets of how to draw a classic Disney character.
- Sorcerer's Workshop: Enjoy lots of hands on fun
- Character Close-Up: See three-dimensional versions of your favorite Toy Story characters..
- Turtle Talk with Crush - This interactive show with everybody's favorite turtle from Finding Nemo, who appears on the screen to look at all "the humans in the human tank". Through some amazing technology, Crush is able to interact with the children in the audience.

Disney Junior Live on Stage! - Sing, dance and play in this 24-minute stage show with your Disney Junior friends. Stars of the Disney Channel's popular Disney Junior take to the stage in this fun-filled show, with sing-alongs and dance activities. In addition to the fun special effects (bubbles and confetti rain down on you at various points of the show), youngsters in the audience can join the gang in singing along with catchy tunes and dancing.

Frozen – Live at the Hyperion - Delight in the magic of Frozen like never before in an all-new, larger-than-life stage production. The show brings Anna, Elsa, Kristoff, Sven and everyone's favorite snowman Olaf to life on stage.

Dining

Award Wieners - LD $ - Counter Service - Mobile Order - Hot dogs and gourmet sausages.

Studio Catering Co. S $ - Counter Service - Sandwiches, salads, chips and cold beverages. Open seasonally.

Fairfax Market – S $ - Fresh fruit, healthy vegetables with dip, deli-style sandwiches, Strawberries with dipping sauce, trail mix, dill pickles and cold beverages.

Schmoozies – S $ - Fresh Fruit Smoothies!

Shopping

Gone Hollywood – This Art Deco themed shop features Star Wars and Marvel merchandise.

Tower Hotel Gifts - Tower of Terror merchandise.

Off the Page – Features Disney collectibles, animation cels, limited edition prints, books, tapes, DVDs, and other souvenirs. The fun décor is worth a visit. On the ceiling are sketches with the characters literally falling "off the page."

Studio Store – This shop features Frozen and other merchandise.

Cars Land

Enter Radiator Springs to spend time with all your favorites from the *Cars* movies.

Attractions

Luigi's Rollickin' Roadsters - Luigi's tire yard has turned into a dance floor and guests can ride along with Luigi's cousins. Each vehicle has a distinct personality and signature dance moves, making each ride different from the last.

Mater's Junkyard Jamboree - This ride is a tractor-pulling square dance hosted by Mater. Guests will be pulled along in trailers as they swing to music by Mater.

Radiator Springs Racers *(FP)(H40)* - Six-passenger vehicles will go on a fast paced adventure through Radiator Springs and see all of its famous residents. The ride concludes with a side-by-side race to the finish line.

Dining

Cozy Cones BLD $ - Counter Service - Serves cone-themed snacks. Offers churro or pretzel bites, soft serve ice cream, "route" beer floats, flavored popcorn, plus edible bread cones filled with bacon and scrambled eggs for breakfast and chicken verde, chili "cone" queso, or bacon mac n' cheese for lunch and dinner.

Fillmore's Taste-In S $ - Counter Service – Enjoy fresh fruit, bottled water, juices and soft drinks.

Flo's V8 Cafe BLD $$ - Counter Service - Mobile Order - Features food inspired by cafes along Route 66. Flo serves comfort food including hot sandwiches, rotisserie chicken, and BBQ pork ribs with Coca Cola BBQ.

Shopping

Sarge's Surplus Hut – A wide selection of merchandise featuring Lightning McQueen and Tow Mater, kids clothing, costumes, hats toys and plush toys.

Ramone's House of Body Art - Features clothing and accessories to help you hit the road in style.

Radiator Springs Curios - Features souvenirs for the road: "Cars" themed pins and vinylmation, plus antenna toppers, window clings, license plate frames and magnets.

Pacific Wharf

This area is solely dedicated to dining. The area represents the waterfronts of Monterey and San Francisco.

Attractions

Bakery Tour - See how San Francisco's famous Boudin sourdough bread is made fresh here at the Pacific Wharf. Bread is baked daily, and guests can taste a sample at the beginning of the tour. The bread is used for Disneyland Resort's bread bowl soups and guests can purchase loaves.

Dining

Ghirardelli Soda Fountain and Chocolate Shop - S $ - Counter Service - Satisfy your sweet tooth for hot fudge sundaes and other ice cream specialties at the soda fountain or take home some famous Ghirardelli Squares from the chocolate shop.

Pacific Wharf Cafe – BLD $ - Counter Service - Mobile Order - Choose from the healthy variety of food, including fresh-baked bread, fresh garden salads, soups in a bread bowl, and other baked goods.

Cocina Cucamonga Mexican Grill – LD $$ - Counter Service - Mobile Order - Serves a mix of Californian and Mexican cuisine, featuring chicken and carne asada tacos, carnitas, burritos, nachos, salads.

Lucky Fortune Cookery – LD $ - Counter Service - Mobile Order - Features chicken, beef and tofu rice bowls including a selection of sauces.

Wine Country Trattoria, at the Golden Vine Winery – LD $$$ - Table Service - The Golden Vine Winery features the Four separate areas: Wine

Country Trattoria, Mendocino Terrace, Sonoma Terrace and Alfresco Tasting Terrace.

- Wine Country Trattoria - Italian food is served inside the dining room or out on the terrace for lunch or dinner. Delicious Italian cuisine featuring lasagna, pastas, grilled sandwiches, and soups. The terrace overlooks the Pacific Wharf and Paradise Pier areas. Priority Seating is available. Reservations can be made by calling 714-781-DINE. Walk-ups are not permitted.
- Alfresco Tasting Terrace - Enjoy your favorite wines along with small Italian-inspired appetizers on the second-floor terrace overlooking Cars Land's Ornament Valley.
- Mendocino Terrace – Wine sampling that's overseen by a wine expert. You can buy wine by the glass or bottle, and enjoy your selection at the counter or under the shady trees of the plaza. The experts are there to answer your questions about the products offered.
- Sonoma Terrace - Sample of diverse selection of craft beer, plus enjoy gourmet meat and cheese plates.
- Alfresco Tasting Terrace - Enjoy your favorite wines along with small Italian-inspired appetizers on the second-floor terrace overlooking Cars Land's Ornament Valley.

Pacific Warf Distribution Co. S$ – Beer and snacks

Rita Baja Blenders S$ - Frozen margaritas in strawberry or lemon-lime

Shopping

Ghirardelli Soda Fountain and Chocolate Shop - Take home some famous Ghirardelli Squares from the chocolate shop.

Paradise Gardens Park

Disney's tribute to the carnivals, amusement parks and boardwalks of old. Plenty of old-fashioned fun.

Attractions

Golden Zephyr - Takes you for a spin over Paradise Bay. The metallic spaceship looking ride vehicles were inspired by classic sci-fi stories such as Buck Rogers and Flash Gordon.

Jumpin' Jellyfish *(H40)* - Head "under the sea" and float like a jellyfish on this kid-friendly parachute ride. You'll soar 40 feet in the air and float back down through the colorful kelp garden.

Goofy's Sky School *(FP)(H42)* - Inspired by the 1940 cartoon short, "Goofy's Glider", this reimagined coaster follows Goofy's attempts to teach a group of novice pilots how to fly.

The Little Mermaid - Ariel's Undersea Adventure - Ride in your own clamshell to follow Ariel and her friends through the scenes of the Little Mermaid. After getting into your 2+ person clamshell you'll descend under the sea in this recreation of the new classic Disney movie. You'll hear all the famous songs too. As the ride nears the end you'll surface and see Ariel.

Silly Symphony Swings *(H40)* – A classic carnival ride, the swings spin around in a circle as you swing outward.

Dining

Bayside Brews – S$ - Mobile Order - Pretzels, draft beer and drinks

Boardwalk Pizza & Pasta - LD $ - Counter Service - Flat bread pizzas, pastas and freshly-tossed salads.

Paradise Garden Grill - LD $ - Counter Service – Features Mediterranean-inspired skewers with various sauces plus classic Greek salads.

Corn Dog Castle – S$ - Counter Service - Mobile Order - Regular and spicy corn dogs, cheese sticks, drinks.

Shopping

Seaside Souvenirs - Hats, pins, World of Color merchandise

Pixar Pier

Discover a Whimsical Boardwalk Where Pixar Stories and Characters Come to Life!

Attractions

Toy Story Midway Mania - Try to get the most points on this 4D shootin' arcade ride. The targets and weapons vary, from rings to darts to baseballs.

Incredicoaster *(FP)(H48)* - Go from 0 to 55 miles per hour in 4.7 seconds. Swoop, swirl, dip and curl in and around Pixar Pier with the epic Parr family. This awesome ride will take you through twists and turns, with a 108 foot drop and an upside down loop!

Games of the Pixar Pier - A midway type area filled with old-fashioned games of luck, chance and skill. There is a separate charge to play any of the midway games, usually $2.50 per game. Prizes are awarded.

Jessie's Critter Carousel - Jessie the yodeling cowgirl invites you for a rootin' tootin' spin on Jessie's Critter Carousel. Saddle up on one of 56 adorable friends, choosing from a turtle, snake, buzzard, armadillo, bunny, deer, raccoon, ram, skunk and two cozy logs inhabited by a family of owls.

Pixar Pal-A-Round swinging gondolas – A new take on the Ferris wheel. It offers spectacular views of the park. There are two types of gondolas and two separate lines. The stationary gondolas do not rock, the swinging gondolas slide around on a circular track and rock back and forth as the wheel spins. Each of the gondolas—swinging and non-swinging—is delightfully decorated with the image of a different Disney Pixar movie character.

Inside Out Emotional Whirlwind – Coming Soon...

Dining

Lamplight Lounge LD $$ - Table Service – The upstairs lounge offers appetizers and drinks, with shareable menu options including potato skins, tuna poke, carne asada rolls and the ultimate Guest-favorite, lobster nachos. The downstairs dining area offers spinach salad, salmon PLT (pancetta, lettuce and tomato), chicken sandwich, cheddar burger, or savory ratatouille. *Reservations Highly Suggested!*

Adorable Snowman Frosted Treats - S $ - Soft Serve and frozen parfait.

Angry Dogs - S $ - Hot Dogs.

Jack Jack Cookie Num Nums – S $ - Cookies and milk.

Poultry Place – S $ - Turkey legs, chicken legs, and corn

Señor Buzz Churros – S $ - Churros

Shopping

Knick's Knacks - A variety of Pixar merchandise

Grizzly Peak

Grizzly Peak resembles a Northern Californian gold mining operation. The centerpiece of this section is Grizzly Peak, a 110 foot high bear shaped mountain that is home to the Grizzly River Run attraction.

Attractions

Grizzly River Run *(FP H42)* - Grizzly River Run is a white water raft ride. The six-passenger rafts start with a 45-foot high climb up Grizzly

Peak. There are two drops, the final one being the Grizzly-Go-Round. Guests drop 22 feet, while the raft spins 360°. Large amounts of water can come into the raft!!! There is an elevated foot rail to keep your feet off the floor. Count on someone in the raft (not everyone) getting very, very wet!

Redwood Creek Challenge Trail - This is a huge children's play area set in the California redwoods. There are plenty of fun things for kids to do along the trail. *(H42 for the Rock Climb and zip-line)*

Soarin' Around The World *(FP)(H40)* - Fly over scenic world destinations on this hang-glider simulator. Each section of this huge simulator has three long rows of seats. You will strap into your seat and then be lifted up into the air where you will be suspended in front of a huge wide screen upon which the flyover scenes are displayed. Try to notice the scents that accompany many of the scenes! Your seat will move and sway in tune with the video to strengthen the feeling of flying.

Dining

Smokejumpers Grill - BLDS $$ - Counter Service - Mobile Order - Features top-your-own burgers, fries, ribs, grilled chicken sandwiches, salad, onion rings.

Shopping

Rushin' River Outfitters - Features clothing, postcards, maps, books, and outdoor related souvenirs. You can buy ponchos here to keep dry on the Grizzly River Run.

Humphrey's Service & Supplies - Clothing and hats for kids, plus Smokey Bear and other forest related merchandise.

California Adventure Entertainment

Nighttime Shows

World of Color *(FP)* – "Mixed Media" (water projected images, lasers, lighting effects, and fireworks) set in time to music make this an awesome show. This is another good vs. evil storyline featuring many of your favorite Disney characters. Depending on the wind, those standing up close could get wet from the water mist used for projections.

Parades

Paint the Night - An after-dark sensation that ignites the night with electrifying enchantment. Sorcerer Mickey is the star of the show, leading the way while conjuring up glittering visions with a wave of his hand. Watch Tinker Bell paint rainbows with pinches of pixie dust—right before your eyes.

Final thoughts on the Disney's California Adventure

Disney's California Adventure has made great strides in recent years with new attractions and lands and now rivals the original park in the breadth of things to experience.

Touring Disney World's Parks

Prior to 2017 military families typically used the highly discounted 3-day Disney Armed Forces Salute tickets. This allowed you to either spend a full day in each park while splitting the third day or to do two days in one park and one day in the other. Now since 2017 with the addition of the 4-day Disney Armed Forces Salute tickets military guests get to spend two days in each park!

Military Disney Tips

- It is so convenient to hop between the two parks. The gates are literally steps from each other. This is a big culture shift for those used to having to take motorized transportation between Florida's Disney parks. It is so easy to pop back and forth between the two. I love it!
- While touring the Disneyland park you can pop over to California Adventure for a lunch or dinner with adult beverages, then head back for more fun for the kids.

Wrap Up

You can see that Disneyland's theme parks have a lot to offer. You will find things that interest every member of the family both young and not so young. It is important to have a good idea what you'd like to accomplish prior to starting each day so that you don't lose time floundering and backtracking your steps across the park.

Ready for More?

I hope that you have enjoyed our whirlwind tour of the Disneyland Resort's theme parks.

Our next chapter covers the technologies that are available to help you plan and manage your Disneyland vacation.

7. Disneyland's Technology

What's This Chapter About?

This chapter is all about the technology that Disneyland offers to improve their guest's experience. From rider reservations to taking pictures for you, Disney has you covered.

FastPass

FastPass is a free service offered at Disneyland, which allows theme park guests to make reservations ahead of time for many of Disneyland's attractions, shows, and experiences.

You do so by obtaining a FastPass ticket from a dispenser nearby the desired attraction. After inserting a valid theme park ticket a FastPass ticket is issued from a slot on the dispenser.

FastPasses are issued for a one-hour block of time in the future. When you return during that time period you will enter the attraction through a line with a negligible to short wait time compared to the normal standby line.

As the day progresses, return times get later and later until all return times have been issued and FastPasses for that attraction will be done for the day.

All members of your party must have their own FastPass ticket to use the FastPass entrance. But one person (a FastPass Runner) can take everyone's tickets to the dispenser to get the FastPasses while the rest of the party does other things (bathroom break, orders food, rests, etc.).

While you are waiting for your FastPass return time you may do anything else that you'd like, such as riding another attraction, dining, or shopping.

After obtaining a FastPass, you may not get another until either you have entered the return time window on your current FastPass or it has been 2 hours since your current FastPass has been issued.

FastPass Attractions

Disneyland Park

- Big Thunder Mountain Railroad
- Buzz Lightyear Astro Blasters
- Haunted Mansion
- Indiana Jones Adventure
- It's a small world
- Matterhorn Bobsleds
- Roger Rabbit's Car Toon Spin
- Space Mountain
- Splash Mountain
- Star Tours: The Adventures Continue
- Fantasmic nighttime show

Disney California Adventure

- Goofy's Sky School
- Grizzly River Run
- Guardians of the Galaxy – Mission: BREKOUT!
- Incredicoaster
- Radiator Springs Racers
- Soarin' Over California
- Toy Story Manina
- World of Color nighttime show

World of Color FastPasses are for reserved viewing sections, not times. This spreads the crowd out through the best viewing locations. You can obtain the World of Color FastPasses near Grizzly River Run.

FastPasses for shows like World of Color and Fantasmic do not count against your one at a time FastPass limit.

Max Pass

Disneyland's MaxPass, allows guests to maximize their experience by enabling the convenience of mobile booking and redemption of Disney FastPass return times by using the Disneyland App and by providing unlimited downloads of their high-resolution PhotoPass images (see PhotoPass info further below).

Disney MaxPass is available for $10 a day. Disneyland Resort Annual Pass holders also have the opportunity to purchase Disney MaxPass on a daily or yearly basis ($75 per year).

The free Disneyland smartphone app is required to use this service. Make you FastPasses without going to the attraction and then scan the code from the app to redeem your FastPass at the correct timeslot.

Guests will continue to have the option of the standard Disney FastPass service at no cost by obtaining FastPasses at attraction FastPass kiosks, just as they have always done.

Disneyland Smartphone App

Disneyland has a smart phone app that has quite a few useful features. Using the app can make your day much more efficient. I particularly like the attraction wait time feature.

The app has a GPS map showing your current location. You can scroll, expand and contract the scale to see just what you need. The map interface has different tabs which in turn display:

- Attraction wait times, descriptions, and accessibility info with the ability to filter by location, thrill factor, and age
- FastPass Return times currently being issued for some attractions
- Character locations and times
- Dining locations, information, and menus
- The ability to make dining reservations
- Mobile food ordering at designated locations
- Merchandise locations and information
- Restroom locations!

There are also sections for:

- Scheduled Park Hours
- Current Day Park schedules and info
- Dining – Reservations, locations, and menus (parks, hotels, and Downtown Disney)
- Buy Theme Park Tickets
- Link Annual Passes to use your phone as your ticket
- Link your PhotoPass account and view your pics

Disney's PhotoPass

PhotoPass is Disney's program for having their professional photographers document your Disneyland Vacation.

Almost everywhere you go in the Disney theme parks, you'll see Disney PhotoPass Photographers. They are stationed at all of the best, most scenic locations to take your picture, for example in front of Sleeping Beauty Castle.

There are also photographers at some of the character meals, at Character Meet and Greets, and many thrill rides also have automatic cameras to capture your reactions to the most thrilling part of the ride.

Taking the photos is a free service, you can decide later if you want to purchase the photos. Just have your PhotoPass ticket scanned to identify who you are and get your picture taken.

You can then review your photos using your Disneyland mobile app or online at the PhotoPass site.

PhotoPass Attractions:

At Disneyland Park:

- Space Mountain
- Splash Mountain

At Disney California Adventure Park:

- California Screamin'
- Radiator Springs Racers

Near the exits of each of these attractions, a preview wall lets you view the picture taken of your recent experience. You can link your 8-character Attraction ID, located on the preview wall, to your Disney account with the Disneyland mobile app or by visiting Disneyland.com/PhotoPass.

PhotoPass Dining Locations:

- Ariel's Grotto in Disney California Adventure Park
- Disney's PCH Grill in Disney's Paradise Pier Hotel
- Goofy's Kitchen in The Disneyland Hotel
- Plaza Inn in Disneyland Park

You can also link your dining photos to your Disney account with your Disneyland mobile app or by visiting Disneyland.com/PhotoPass.

PhotoPass Collection

Disneyland also has a product that they call the PhotoPass Collection. This product includes:

- Digital downloads of all Disney PhotoPass photos in your account at time of redemption
- A voucher for a Dining Print Package (Voucher may not be redeemed online. See voucher for restrictions.)
- A Disneyland Resort Gallery Disc, featuring more than 350 high-resolution professional photos from around Disneyland Resort

For 2018 and 2019 the Disney Armed Forces Salute offers a special military price on the Collection.

You can purchase the new Disney PhotoPass Collection product for a discounted price- $49 plus tax through December 19, 2018 and January 1, 2019 – December 19, 2019.

The Disney PhotoPass Collection product can only be purchased at the following Disneyland Resort merchandise locations, by eligible service members or their spouses.

- Main Street Photo Supply Co. at Disneyland Park
- Kingswell Camera Shop at Disney California Adventure Park

How purchasing pictures works

You can either purchase your photos a la carte after the fact or purchase a prepaid day or weeklong package.

Photos may be purchased as individual digital downloads. Or if you have purchased a Disney PhotoPass+ One Day or One Week, all your attraction photos captured during the day(s) of your activation window are included. If you have a Disney Signature or Disney Signature Plus Passport, all your attraction photos are included for the duration of your passport.

Disney PhotoPass photos expire 45 days after capture, but a one-time Expiration Extension allows you to have 60 days after capture to view your photos and decide which ones you want.

Regular Prices:

Prepaid PhotoPass+ costs $39 plus tax for the One Day and $78 plus tax the One Week versions. The expiration extension is $19.95 plus tax.

For this price you'll receive unlimited digital downloads of all the pictures you had taken on your vacation for up to 45 days afterwards, a CD backup can be purchased for an extra fee.

When purchasing a la carte you can download any of the pictures that you select, which were taken of you on your vacation. You'll pay $14.95 each photo though.

Military Disney Tips

- Make sure to bring your own charging pack for your devices (available cheaply on Amazon). With no WiFi in the parks your battery will drain before the end of the day if you are using the Disneyland app to any extent.
- I highly recommend using the Disneyland Park app to check wait times and make dining reservations on the fly!

Wrap up

That's it for right now, but you can count on Disney to keep innovating and creating new tech to improve our vacations.

Ready for More?

Our next chapter is the General dining chapter, where we'll do an overview of your dining options at Disneyland and then talk about ways that you can save some on this pricey vacation item.

8. Disneyland Dining

What's This Chapter About?

This is our general dining chapter where you'll get an overview of the types of dining options at Disneyland, the discounts that are available for dining, and some ways to economize on your food costs.

You'll find the listings of specific restaurants within the chapters pertaining to where they are located, those being the Theme Park, Resorts, and Other Entertainment chapters.

The range of dining options at Disneyland is absolutely fantastic! There is everything available from grab and go locations, to Starbucks, counter service, sit down dining, and even signature dining. You can even dine with your favorite Disney character.

There is something for every taste and budget!

Dining Terms at Disneyland

Any discussion of dining at Disneyland requires the use a few Disney terms that Disney uses in regards to dining.

Disney classifies their restaurants by how the food is served, here are the Disney terms and what they mean.

- Quick Service – These are dining locations at which you wait in line to order your food at a counter, window, or freestanding cash register. You then wait for your food and carry it to the table of your choice.

- Table Service - These are dining locations at which you are seated at a table by a host or hostess and a waitress or waiter takes your order and delivers your food.
- Family Style - These are dining locations at which you are seated at a table by a host or hostess and a waitress or waiter takes your order and delivers your food. These locations may have one set menu or a variety that you can choose from. In either case, your food will be delivered to the table on platters and in serving bowls. Your family will then fix their own plates from the serving dishes. These locations are usually "All You Care to Eat."
- Buffet Service - These are dining locations at which you are seated at a table by a host or hostess and a waitress or waiter takes your drink order. You'll then go to the buffet area to fill your own plates, these meals are "All You Care to Eat."
- All You Care to Eat – Disney for "All You Can Eat", used in conjunction with Family Style and Buffet Meals.

Disney Dining Overview

Reservations

Most Disneyland Table Service restaurants accept Advance Dining Reservations or ADRs. ADRs are slightly different from the reservations you are used to in the non-Disney World.

An Advance Dining Reservation time, is a time at which you should be present at the restaurant (Disney recommends arriving 15 minutes early). When you arrive you'll check in and then be placed in the queue for the next available table. There may be others both with and without ADRs in this queue ahead of you.

Advance Dining Reservations are recommended even in the slower times of the year, especially for popular restaurants!

A credit card is required at the time you make your ADR and there is a fee that will be charged for same day cancellations. You may only make one ADR per meal. The single ADR requirement and cancellation fee are due to the fact that in the past there were those who made multiple ADRs per meal at different locations to "cover their bases" no matter where they wound up they'd have a place to eat.

Advance Dining Reservations may be made 60 days in advance.

Reserve online or by calling (714) Disneyland-DINE or (714) 781-3463.

Character Meals

At Disneyland you have the ability to meet and greet various Disney Characters during your meal at certain locations. Different restaurants feature different characters.

Character meals are served a couple different ways depending on which restaurant you choose.

- Traditional buffet-style -- available at most of the participating restaurants.
- Family-style -- the server brings large bowls/plates/skillets of food that you serve yourself and pass around the table.

As a rule, you need to make Advance Reservations for character meals. However, during slow seasons it is sometimes possible to attend a Character Meal without an Advance Reservation. Advance Reservations are available for all character meals and can be arranged by calling (714) Disneyland-DINE or (714) 781-3463.

Character Meals by Location:

Disneyland Park

Plaza Inn - B$$ - Buffet Service – (Minnie and rotating characters) Meet the characters during breakfast which features a variety of breakfast items on the buffet.

Disney's California Adventure

Ariel's Grotto - BL$$$ - Table Service Fixed Price – (Ariel and rotating Princesses) Breakfast offers a selection of single meals to accompany the pastry and fruit starter at your table. For lunch and dinner select from roast chicken, barbeque tri-tip, grilled lobster salad, or catch of the day, among others.

Disneyland Resorts

Disney's PCH Grill – Paradise Pier Hotel - B$$ - Buffet Service – (Donald and rotating characters) Meet the characters during breakfast which features a variety of breakfast items on the buffet.

Goofy's Kitchen – Disneyland Hotel – BD$$$ - Buffet Service – (Goofy and rotating characters) Breakfast offerings are typical buffet items accompanied by specialty hot beverages if desired and brunch style cocktails are also available. Dinner offerings include: carving station, catch of the day, veggies, salads, fruit, Pluto's hot dogs, pizza, Goofyroni & cheese, desserts, soft serve yogurt.

Storytellers Café – Grand Californian Hotel – B$$ - Buffet/Table Service – (Mickey and other rotating characters) Cooked to order omelets and other traditional breakfast items are in store during the morning buffet.

Dining Packages

Fantasmic - Disneyland offers Fantasmic Dining Packages, which combine a "Prix Fixe" meal (a meal consisting of several courses for a fixed price) and entry to a preferred viewing area for Fantasmic.

Included with each Fantasmic Dining Package meal:

- Table Service 3-course meal (starter, entree, and dessert) from a set menu during lunch and/or dinner depending on the restaurant. Plus a non-alcoholic beverage.
- One voucher for the preferred Fantasmic viewing area.

Dining Locations

- Blue Bayou - $62.00 adult/$29.00 child (3-9) plus tax (themed Fantasmic seat cushion included)
- River Belle Terrace - $45.00 adult/$25.00 child (3-9) plus tax
- Hungry Bear Restaurant - $29.99 adult/$19.99 child (3-9) plus tax (this package includes a boxed grab and go meal with dessert and drink)

Paint the Night - Disneyland offers Paint the Night Dining Packages, which combine a "Prix Fixe" meal and entry to a preferred viewing area for Paint the Night.

Included with each Paint the Night Dining Package meal:

- Table Service 3 or 4 course meal from a set menu during lunch and/or dinner depending on the restaurant. Plus a non-alcoholic beverage.
- One voucher for the preferred Fantasmic viewing area.

Dining Locations

- Carthay Circle Restaurant - $99.00 adult/$45.00 child (3-9) plus tax (4-course dinner)

- Wine Country Trattoria - $49.00 adult/$25.00 child (3-9) plus tax (3-course lunch or dinner)

Frozen - California Adventure offers the Frozen Dining Package, which combine a "Prix Fixe" meal and priority seating for Frozen – Live at the Hyperion.

Included with each Frozen Package meal:

- Table Service 3-course meal from a set menu during lunch and/or dinner depending on the restaurant. Plus a non-alcoholic beverage.
- One voucher for priority seating.

Dining Locations

- Carthay Circle Restaurant - $89.00 adult/$45.00 child (3-9) plus tax (lunch)

World of Color - Disneyland also offers World of Color Dining Packages, which combine a "Prix Fixe" meal and entry to a preferred viewing area for the World of Color performance. *Note: World of Color is closed through late 2018.*

Included with each World of Color Dining Package meal:

- Table Service 3-course meal (starter, entree, and dessert) from a set menu during lunch and/or dinner depending on the restaurant. Plus a non-alcoholic beverage.
- One voucher for the preferred World of Color viewing area.

Dining Locations (prices and locations are for 2018. 2019 is TBD)

- Lamplight Lounge (expected to replace Ariel's Grotto)

- o   Dinner - $49.00 adult/$25.00 child (3-9) includes tax
- o   Dinner - $49.00 adult/$25.00 child (3-9) includes tax
- Wine Country Trattoria
  - o   Lunch - $38.00 adult/$21.00 child
  - o   Dinner - $49.00 adult/$25.00 child
- Carthay Circle Restaurant
  - o   Lunch - $46.00 adult/$25.00 child
  - o   Dinner - $62.00 adult/$25.00 child

(Prices subject to change)

Space is limited, so reservations are highly recommended.

Disneyland Dining Discounts

No Disney Military Dining Discounts

Unfortunately, while Disney offers great military discounts on their resort rooms and theme park tickets, they do not offer any military discounts on dining!

But don't worry, there are other discounts and options that you can take advantage of.

Disneyland Passholders

Disneyland Passholders receive Disneyland dining discounts at many Disneyland restaurants. The list is long and ever changing, so be sure to ask before ordering! At Disneyland the servers are actually very good about asking if you are a passholder.

Save 10 to 15 percent (depending on pass type and restaurant) off of regularly priced food and non-alcoholic beverages at select Disneyland

Resort Table-Service locations. See a list of participating restaurants at the end of this chapter.

Disney Visa Card Holders

Disney Visa Rewards Card holders receive Disneyland dining discounts at select Disneyland restaurants. The list is nowhere near as long as the passholder list. Be sure to ask before ordering!

Save 10 percent off of regularly priced food and non-alcoholic beverages at select Disneyland Resort Table-Service locations. See a list of participating restaurants at the end of this chapter.

Downtown Disney Restaurant's Military Discounts

There are several non-Disney owned restaurants at Disneyland's Downtown Disney that do offer military discounts!

Here are the restaurants and their discounts.

Catal Restaurant & Uva Bar/Lounge - 10% Military Discount

Naples Ristorante e Pizzeria - 10% Military Discount

Ralph Brennan's Jazz Kitchen - 10% Military Discount

La Brea Bakery 10%

Earl of Sandwich - 10% Military Discount

Ghirardelli Chocolate Company - 10% Military Discount

Rainforest Cafe - 10% Military Discount (currently closed)

Don't just ask for a military discount at these locations, ask wherever you go! At locations where they do not offer one, cast members have been known to give you their employee discount just to say thanks. They do this without mentioning it, but you can see they did by checking the receipt for Cast Discount.

Note: these military discount locations and amounts are subject to change.

Other Ways to Save

Bring and eat your own food. The Disney Hotels have mini-fridges in their rooms. You can keep some basic items for breakfast and snacks, or even for lunch in the parks.

There are several ways that you can stock your room stash:

- Bring your food with you (if driving)
- Coordinate a grocery stop with your limo service (if flying)
- Have food pre-delivered to your resort by GardenGrocer.com or WeGoShop.com
- Buy items at your resort's sundries shop

Disney allows you to bring food and drinks into the parks. You can do so in backpacks or soft coolers, no hard coolers or glass items are allowed.

During a bag check at Florida's Epcot I was once behind a family of four where both the mom and dad had a backpack almost busting open they were so full. When they opened them up for the security bag check tons of food, paper plates, and plasticware came spilling out, there was a whole very large cooked chicken in one! It looked like they could have fed three families with all they had…

That was a little overboard, but some snacks, sandwiches and drinks will get you through your theme park day.

More Tips

Share meals. Disney portions are often very large. To reduce costs share entrees and appetizers rather that getting one for everyone.

Kid's meals. Order the cheaper Kid's Meal at Quick Service restaurants (if they appeal).

Free soda, coffee, and tea refills. You will find that very few Quick Service restaurants at Disneyland offer free refills. But there are a few in the theme parks and at Downtown Disney which do.

Cups of water/ice. All Disney Quick Service restaurants will give you a cup of ice or cup of water (tap water vs. a water bottle) for free. You can just get the water for everyone (It will help with your hydration!) or you can get one large soda and cups of ice to split up the soda. In Table Service locations opt for tap water.

Eat off Disney property.

There are several restaurants along Disneyland Drive to the east of the Esplanade area that are within a quarter of a mile.

- Panera Bread
- McDonalds
- The Pizza Press
- Cove on the Harbor Market and Cafe
- IHOP
- Cold Stone Creamery
- Denny's
- Tony Romas

Just a little further (about a third of a mile) is the north entrance to the Anaheim Garden Walk with more dining and shopping options

- House of Blues (20% military discount)

- Bubba Gimp Shrimp
- PF Changs
- California Pizza Kitchen
- The Cheesecake Factory
- And More…

Passholder Dining Discount Participating Restaurants

Subject to change

Disneyland Park

Alien Pizza Planet
Bengal Barbecue
Blue Bayou Restaurant
Cafe Orleans
Carnation Café
Clarabelle's
Daisy's Diner
French Market Restaurant
Galactic Grill
Harbour Galley
Hungry Bear Restaurant
Jolly Holiday Bakery Café
Market House
Plaza Inn
Pluto's Dog House
Rancho del Zocalo Restaurante
Red Rose Tavern
Refreshment Corner
River Belle Terrace
Royal Street Veranda

Stage Door Café
The Golden Horseshoe
Troubadour Tavern

Disney's California Adventure

Alfresco Tasting Terrace
Award Wieners
Boardwalk Pizza & Pasta
Carthay Circle Lounge
Carthay Circle Restaurant
Cocina Cucamonga Mexican Grill
Corn Dog Castle
Fiddler, Fifer & Practical Café
Flo's V8 Café
Ghirardelli® Soda Fountain and Chocolate Shop
Lamplight Lounge
Lucky Fortune Cookery
Mendocino Lounge
Pacific Wharf Café
Paradise Garden Grill
Smokejumpers Grill
Sonoma Terrace
Studio Catering Co.
Wine Country Trattoria

Disney's Grand Californian Hotel & Spa

Hearthstone Lounge
Storytellers Café
White Water Snacks

Disney's Paradise Pier Hotel

Disney's PCH Grill
Surfside Lounge

Disneyland Hotel

Goofy's Kitchen
Steakhouse 55
Tangaroa Terrace
Trader Sam's Enchanted Tiki Bar

Downtown Disney District

Catal Restaurant
Earl of Sandwich
Jamba Juice
Kayla's Cake
La Brea Bakery Café & Express
Naples Ristorante e Pizzeria
Napolini
Ralph Brennan's Jazz Kitchen & Express
Splitsville Juxury Lanes
Sprinkles
Taqueria at Tortilla Jo's
Tortilla Jo's
Uva Bar
Wetzel's Pretzels
Tortilla Jo's

Disney Visa Dining Discount Participating Restaurants

Disneyland Park

French Market
River Belle Terrace

Disney California Adventure Park

Cocina Cucamonga Mexican Grill
Wine Country Trattoria
Paradise Garden Grill

Disneyland Resort Hotels

Steakhouse 55
Disney's PCH Grill
Storytellers Café

Military Disney Tips

- If you desire anything more than fast food during your vacation, reservations for Disneyland's restaurants are highly recommended.
- Use your Disneyland Park app to check for restaurants near you with times available.

Wrap up

There is a great variety of dining options available at Disneyland. There is something for every palate and price point. There are even a few military discounts.

You can do a whole vacation just eating on the fly at whatever is convenient at the time, planning out every dining experience using reservations, or a mix. It's all available to you.

Ready for More?

We've hit all the major areas, now it's time to see what else there is to do at Disneyland. In the next chapter we'll cover lots of other things to do on your vacation.

9. Other Things to Do at Disneyland

What's This Chapter About?

So far we've discussed Disneyland's two theme parks, the tickets needed to enter them, dining at Disneyland, and where to stay while you're there.

Now we'll discuss everything else that there is to do at Disneyland and the military discounts that are available for some of them. Some of these things are even free!

We'll also touch on the discounts that are available for Anaheim's other theme parks and entertainment venues.

Downtown Disney

Downtown Disney is Disneyland's shopping and entertainment complex. You'll find great dining options, many merchandise stores (Disney and others), as well as many entertainment venues here.

The merchants at Downtown Disney are a mix of Disney and non-Disney owned locations. While Disney does not offer any military discounts on food or merchandise, some of the non-Disney locations do!

Below you'll find an overview of what Downtown Disney has to offer. Any locations with military discounts are noted.

Note if you are told by your server that one of the locations I mention has no military discount, be sure to speak to a manager to check. The availability of military discounts has been known to change over time and also servers have been known to be wrong. Also feel free to ask about a discount at locations that are not listed as having a military discount, it never hurts!

Note military discounts are subject to change, as are the current list of open locations due to the construction.

Dining

Catal Restaurant and Uva Bar – $$ - American and Mediterranean cuisine. Fine dining in the restaurant and more casual dining outside at the Uva Bar. **(10% Military Discount)**

Earl of Sandwich - $ - Assorted sandwiches, salads, and baked goods. **(10% Military Discount)**

Haagen-Dazs - $ - Gourmet ice cream.

Jamba Juice - $ - Healthy fruit smoothies.

La Brea Bakery - $ - Coffees, pastries, sandwiches, and more. **(10% Military Discount)**

Naples Ristorante e Pizzeria - $$ - Italian specialties including pastas and pizza. **(10% Military Discount)**

Napolini - $ - Quick service location for Naples Ristorante e Pizzeria **(10% Military Discount)**

Ralph Brennan's Jazz Kitchen - $$ - Cajun and Creole menu items. **(10% Military Discount)**

Ralph Brennan's Jazz Kitchen Express - $ - Quick Service Cajun and Creole menu. **(10% Military Discount)**

Splitsville Luxury Lanes - $$ - Upscale entertainment center that combines bowling with billiards, dining, music and nightlife. (Opening winter 2017/2018)

Sprinkles - $ - Bakery Items.

Starbucks – $ - The usual Starbucks stuff. (Two locations)

Tortilla Joes - $$ - Mexican food.

Taqueria at Tortilla Joes - $ - Quick Service Mexican food.

Wetzels Pretzels - $ - All things pretzel.

Note: In mid 2018 Rainforest Café, ESPN Zone, and Earl of Sandwich closed in order to be torn down to make way for a 4th Disney hotel. When construction preparation first started issues were discovered with some of the underlying ground which would have made the construction cost prohibitive. At press time the new hotel has been cancelled and earl of sandwich (listed above) has reopened. The fate of Rainforest Café and ESPN Zone has not been announced!

Rainforest Café – $$ -The national chain offers a unique dining experience that puts you in the middle of an Amazon rainforest. **(10% Military Discount)**

ESPN Zone - $$ - The menu includes typical American fare, including pasta, sandwiches, salads and hamburgers. Sports, Sports, Sports on the TVs, arcade, game day activities, and more. (Disney location, no military discount)

Shopping

Alamo Car Rental

Build-A-Bear Workshop – Your kids can build their own plush bear.

Chapel Hats - Fashionable hats and headwear for guests of all ages. The location carries just about any style of hat including fedoras, sun hats, floppy hats, outdoors hats, kid's hats and more.

Curl Surf – High-end Surf Shop featuring trendy Surf Wear clothing and accessories.

Disney Dress Shop – Disney themed dresses that pay homage to your favorite Disney icons and park attractions.

Disney's Pin Traders - The ultimate pin-purchasing-and-trading location.

Disney Vault 28 – Unique fashion for women and girls.

Dream Boutique – Costumes and character apparel.

D Street - Cutting edge apparel, pop culture novelties, Vinylmation figurines and other collectibles.

The LEGO Store – A huge Lego store.

Marceline's Confectionary – Candy and sweets galore.

Pandora – The jewelry, not the movie with blue aliens.

Ridemakerz – A toy car version of Build a Bear.

Sanuk - Creatively inspired footwear designed with non-traditional materials like yoga-mats.

Sephora – Beauty products.

Sunglass Icon – Sunglasses designed with the athlete, sports and outdoor enthusiast in mind.

WonderGround Gallery – Disney inspired artwork.

World of Disney – A super huge Disney character merchandise store. Clothing, jewelry, home goods, toys, tech needs, etc.

Entertainment

AMC 24 Theatres - 12 separate theaters showing current features and recent Disney films.

ESPN Zone Arcade – 10,000 square foot sports arcade. (Closed at this time)

Splitsville Luxury Lanes - Upscale entertainment center that combines bowling with billiards, dining, music and nightlife. (Coming in 2017)(Disney location, no military discount)

Ralph Brennan's Jazz Kitchen – Flambeaux's Jazz Club – Nightly live entertainment.

Disneyland Tours

Theme Park Tours

Disneyland Resort VIP Tour – The full VIP treatment, a private guide, priority access to 30+ attractions, reserved seating for parades and shows, dining reservations in advance.

Halloween and Christmas Tours – Special tours are offered during these holiday periods. Theme park admission not included.

Call for prices and reservations (714) 300-7710

Backstage Tour

Walk in Walt's Footsteps Guided Tour - Discover what inspired Walt to build his first park. Tour the park and back stage with your guide who will tell stories along the way. Includes lunch or dinner depending on the time in the Main Street USA's Jolly Holiday Bakery. $109 theme park admission not included.

Call (417) 781-8687 for details, pricing, and reservations (which are recommended). You may book 30 days in advance.

Disneyland's Special Halloween Party

Each year Disneyland hosts a special after hours Mickey's Halloween Party. This event is held in the Disneyland Park on select nights from September through October after the regular park hours and require a separate entrance ticket.

Your Disney Armed Forces Salute or regular park tickets will not get you into this party, the purchase of an additional event admission ticket is required to attend.

Disney has never offered a military discount on admission for this party as they do for Mickey's Halloween and Christmas parties in Florida.

Other Non-Disney Theme Parks and Activities

Here are a few of the other activities that are available for you to enjoy during a Disneyland vacation.

Anaheim Garden Walk

Just a short 10-minute walk from the Disney Parks main entrance you'll find the Anaheim Garden Walk mall. This is a great place to pass some time.

Here are some of the dining, shopping, and entertainment options:

Dining

- House of Blues (20% military discount)
- Bubba Gump Shrimp
- PF Changs
- California Pizza Kitchen
- The Cheesecake Factory
- And more…

Shopping

- Skechers
- Los Angeles Harley Davidson
- Sunglass Hut
- And more…

Entertainment

- Bowlmor Lanes
- Mission Escape Games – the new rage, escape rooms
- And more…

Knott's Berry Farm

Is just 7 miles and 15 minutes drive time from Disneyland by car, easily accessible by your car, taxi, or uber or Anaheim Resort Transportation.

See the Transportation Chapter for more

There are plenty of rides and coasters here. Military discounts are offered at the gate (about $30 off) online, or at participating base ticket offices like Camp Pendleton ITT.

Universal Studios Hollywood

Universal Studios is an hour away by car or Anaheim Resort Transportation.

See the Transportation Chapter for more

Universal Studios offers discounted tickets through Base Ticket Offices that you can purchase ahead of time.

If you do not pre-purchase your tickets before arriving, you are still eligible for a discount. Eligible members include active and retired US Military, DOD personnel, National Guard, Reservists and their dependents. Present your valid Military or US Government ID at the ticket booth in order to receive your discount. You will receive a $3.00 discount off General Admission tickets and $3.00 off 48" and below tickets.

SeaWorld San Diego

SeaWorld San Diego is an hour and a half away by car or Anaheim Resort Transportation.

See the Transportation Chapter for more

The SeaWorld Parks have been offering the Waves of Honor (previously the Anheuser-Busch Here's to the Heroes) program since 2005. This fantastic offer allows a free one day admission to one of their nationwide parks per year to current military members and up to 3 direct dependents.

There have also been seasonal discounts or free offers for retirees and veterans (usually November through December in conjunction with Veteran's Day).

See a participating base ticket office, like Camp Pendleton ITT.

Military Disney Tips

- The convenience of Downtown Disney to both the Disney
  Hotels and the theme parks is awesome! It is so easy to walk
  there for dining or shopping. You can even pop out of the parks
  for lunch!
- Catch a movie at the AMC Theatres on a rainy afternoon or
  evening.

Wrap Up

Well, that's it for our other things to do chapter. As you can see there is a
lot more to do on your Disneyland vacation besides just the two theme
parks.

Ready for More?

Well, now you know everything that there is to do at Disneyland, now
you just need to know how to get there. Next we'll cover all the different
transportation options for Disneyland, both how to get there, and then
getting around once you are there.

10. Transportation for your Disneyland Vacation

What's This Chapter About?

This chapter is all about getting to and getting around Disneyland. Before we close the chapter we'll talk about getting to the other area theme parks and transporting the little ones around on your vacation (strollers).

But first you've got to get to Disneyland. There are two main ways that you'll travel to Disneyland, driving or flying. We'll cover both.

Prices in this chapter are subject to change.

Getting to Disneyland

Driving

Many people elect to drive their privately owned vehicle or a rental to Disneyland. There are pluses and minuses to doing so.

Some of the pluses are:

- The ability to drive to other local area attractions.
- Not having to obtain transportation from the airport.
- Being able to make trips for groceries and supplies.
- The ability to dine off property.
- Bringing more stuff.
- Cheaper than flying.

Some of the minuses are:

- Potentially adding extra days to your vacation.

- Parking costs at hotels depending on where you stay.

The Cost of Parking Your POV

Parking Fees - Depending on where you stay, you might be responsible for paying parking fees.

Disney Hotel Guests – Parking is $20 at your Disneyland Hotel.

Non-Disney Guests - Check with your off property hotel for their specifics.

Disney Theme Park parking is $20 a day.

Flying to Los Angeles and Disneyland

There are several different airports that you could choose from when flying to the Disneyland Resort. The Los Angeles area has several airports: Los Angeles International (commonly called LAX), Long Beach, Orange County (John Wayne), and Ontario.

The closest to Disneyland is John Wayne Orange County (SNA) and the next closest is Long Beach (LGB). I've always used John Wayne, which is about a half hour away with good traffic. Traffic can be bad during rush hour! Opt for either of these two airports if you can find good rates.

Getting to Disneyland

Your options for getting to Disneyland are rent a car, take an airport shuttle or limo, Gray Line Disneyland Express Bus, taxi, or Uber.

Rental Car – If you plan on visiting other local destinations besides Disney this might be a good option for your vacation. Take into consideration the cost of parking the car at your hotel (if any) while you won't be using it and how many side trips that you plan to make. Be sure to check for off duty military rates!

Airport Shuttle/Limo – There are numerous shuttle and limo services in the Los Angles area. I like to use Prime Time Shuttle.

What's so great about Prime Time Shuttle? They offer their customers a discount when they book round trip service and a variety of transport options, ranging from a shared shuttle all the way to a limo for luxury services.

Military members are eligible for 10% off of their regular rates! To get this use the special discount code.

There are three ways to book this awesome fare:

Call their call center to book your reservation, by dialing 800-733-8267 and hit 1 for reservations and give this discount code **584813**

Go to www.primetimeshuttle.com. Where it says frequent rider ID, use discount code **MILITARY** and click GO.

Go to militarydisneytips.com/blog/limo/ this will take you straight to a personalized portal that was created just for my readers.

Disneyland Express Bus by Gray Line – Gray Line offers bus service between LAX and John Wayne and Disneyland.

From LAX, Disneyland Resort Express is $30 one way/$48 roundtrip for an adult. Kids go FREE: one child (age 11 and under) is free with each paying adult. Any additional children cost $22 one way/$36 roundtrip.

From SNA, Disneyland Resort Express is $20 one way/$35 roundtrip for an adult. Kids go FREE: one child (age 11 and under) is free with each paying adult. Any additional children cost $15 one way/$26 roundtrip.

 Disneyland Resort Express from the airport – After picking up your luggage at the airport, proceed out to the pickup location:

- At LAX, go to the center island and stand under the overhead green sign. The bus departs frequently.
- At SNA, go outside to the Ground Transportation Center and find the area in front of the ticket booth on your left. The bus departs frequently.

Disneyland Resort Express to the airport – The bus picks up at 17 stops located throughout the Anaheim resort area including the three Disney resorts.

https://dre.coachusa.com/ShuttleReservations/Home

Contact Gray Line directly at (800) 828-6699 for the current schedule.

Taxi – A taxi will cost about $40 one-way to Disneyland from John Wayne and about $80-$100 from LAX.

Uber – For those who like using Uber the ride from John Wayne to Disneyland will be about $20 (UberX) to $35 (UberXL) one-way in non heavy traffic.

Parking

Disney Hotel Parking

Hotel Parking

For an additional fee, the hotels of the Disneyland Resort offer self-parking and valet service for registered hotel Guests. Follow the signs directly to your destination; do not park in the theme park lot.

Rates For Hotel Guests

- Self-parking: $20 per night per vehicle
- Oversized vehicle parking: $25 per night per vehicle
- Valet parking: $30 per night per vehicle

Rates For Guests Visiting a Disneyland Resort Hotel Restaurant or Spa

- Non-registered Guests 3 hours free with validation from these select table-service restaurants: Goofy's Kitchen, Steakhouse 55, Disney's PCH Grill and Storyteller's Café
- 5 hours free validation from Napa Rose and Mandara Spa

Parking for Disneyland Park, Disney California Adventure Park and the Downtown Disney District is not permitted in the hotel parking lots.

Disney Theme Park Parking Garage/Lots

- $20 for cars and motorcycles
- $25 for oversized vehicles, motor homes and tractors without trailers
- $30 for buses and tractors with extended trailers

Preferred Parking at Mickey & Friends Parking Structure

When you're visiting the theme parks, you have the option to park in designated Preferred Parking close to escalators and elevators. Request the Preferred Parking option upon arrival at the Mickey & Friends parking structure and then follow Cast Members who will direct you to your spot.

- $35 for cars

The number and availability of Preferred Parking spaces is limited. Price subject to change at any time.

After parking in the Theme Park lots/structure, you will pass thorough a security check and then board a bus or tram that will take you to the entrance Esplanade area between the theme parks.

Downtown Disney District Parking

The first 23 hours of parking is free in the Downtown Disney District parking lot with a $20 minimum purchase at any Downtown Disney location and a validation. Or up to 5 free hours with validation at AMC Theatres or any table-service dining restaurants. Each additional hour costs $12, charged in 30-minute increments. The maximum parking fee is $48.

Parking for Disneyland Park and Disney California Adventure Park is not permitted in the Downtown Disney lot.

Disability Parking

Parking for Guests with disabilities is available throughout the Disneyland Resort.

Locations include the Mickey & Friends Parking Structure, the Toy Story parking area off Harbor Boulevard, Downtown Disney, and the Resort Hotels. A valid disability-parking permit is required.

Deciding o Drive or Fly

Make sure that when you are comparing the cost of flying to driving, that you include all of the associated costs of each.

For Driving – Hotel, gas, and food costs enroute as well as all tolls and parking fees at Disneyland.

For Flying – Airfare, baggage fees, airport parking or shuttle fees, and meals enroute. Plus any costs for getting to and around Disneyland if any.

Getting Around Disneyland

Driving

Once you have arrived at Disneyland, driving is not required. Disney's three on property hotels are all within walking distance to everything. In fact if you tried to drive to the parks from your Disney hotel, you'd have to park further away and then catch a tram to the parks.

Many off property hotels are also within easy walking distance, some actually are closer than the Disney Hotels!

Walking

Walking is the usual method of getting around at the Disneyland Resort. Walking to the theme parks from your Disneyland Hotel is easy and fairly quick.

There are 3 theme park entrances:

- The Esplanade which is the main entrance location to both parks, located between Disneyland park and California Adventure
- The Grand Californian back entrance to California Adventure
- The Downtown Disney Monorail Station with service to Disneyland Park's Tomorrowland.

Just follow the signs or ask a cast member for directions.

From Paradise Pier to the Theme Parks

Walking Distances:

- Through the Grand Californian
    o To the main theme park entrance – 0.46 miles
    o To the California Adventure rear entrance - 0.30 miles
- Through Downtown Disney
    o To the main theme park entrance – 0.63 miles

    o   To the Downtown Disney Monorail Station - 0.30 miles

From the Disneyland Hotel to the Theme Parks

Walking Distances:

- Through Downtown Disney to the main theme park entrance – 0.46 miles
- To the Downtown Disney Monorail Station – 0.12 miles
- Through Downtown Disney and the Grand Californian to the California Adventure rear entrance – 0.42 miles

From the Grand Californian Hotel and Spa to the Theme Parks

Walking Distances:

- From the lobby through Downtown Disney to the main theme park entry – 0.28 miles
- To the Downtown Disney Monorail Station – 0.22 miles
- From the lobby to the California Adventure rear entrance - 0.10 miles

Resort Shuttle Service

Anaheim Resort Transport (ART) – ART is a local shuttle bus service that connects you to theme parks, hotels, restaurants, shopping, dining and other destinations within the Anaheim Resort area, including the cities of Anaheim, Garden Grove, Buena Park, Costa Mesa, Santa Ana and Orange.

Prices (subject to change):

- 1-Day – Adult $5.50, Kids $2
- 3-Day – Adult $14, Kids $3
- 5-Day – Adult $23, Kids $8

You can purchase tickets at many off property hotel front desks, on their site **rideart.org**, at the kiosk at the Disneyland Resort Main Transportation Center, or use their smart phone mobile app available at the Apple Store and Android Shop (buy passes, get real-time schedules, and keep all your passes in your virtual wallet).

Renting a Car

All the national chains rent cars at the Los Angeles Airports. Be sure to check for military rates or use other discounts for which you might be eligible such as USAA or using points from one of your loyalty programs.

On Disneyland property you can rent from Alamo Rent-A-Car at Downtown Disney near the AMC Theater.

How can I get to Universal Studios or Knotts Berry Farm?

For getting around to the other parks I recommend taking the ART. See the info just above.

Stroller Rentals

Strollers are available for rent from Disney on a daily basis in the Esplanade between the theme parks.

Guests are permitted to bring their own strollers if desired.

Strollers rental fees are $15 per day or $25 per day for two individual strollers.

Stroller rentals are good all day for both parks.

Scooter Rentals

Wheelchairs and Electric Conveyance Vehicles (ECVs or "scooters") are available for rent from Disney on a daily basis in the Esplanade between the theme parks. Quantities are limited and they are available on a first-come-first-serve basis. Guests are permitted to bring their own mobility assistive devices.

Scooter rental fees are $50 per day with an additional $20 refundable deposit. Wheelchairs are $12 per day with a refundable $20 deposit.

Military Disney Tips

- Bring some good walking shoes; you'll be spending a lot of time on your feet!
- Uber is great for getting to nearby off property locations.

Wrap Up

Getting around Disneyland is much easier than its Florida counterpart. Those used to WDW will be surprised at being able to walk everywhere.

Ready for More?

That's it for getting around for most of us, but some of our brethren need just a little more assistance. Next we will cover Disney Disability Information.

11. Disneyland Disability Information

What's This Chapter About?

Many of our brethren are dealing with visible and or invisible reminders of their service to our nation. This chapter outlines Disney's efforts to make these individuals' vacation as smooth as possible.

Disney recently completely overhauled its system for accommodating guests with disabilities.

Here is how the system works and what those with special needs can expect.

Before you arrive

Disney has extensive information for guests with disabilities available on their official website. This should be your first stop when seeking information because it comes directly from the source and does change over time. (See the link at the end of the chapter)

Parking for Guests with Disabilities

Designated parking areas are available throughout Disneyland Resort for Guests with disabilities. A valid disability-parking permit is required.

Theme Park Parking

Guests with the ability to walk short distances and step onto courtesy trams should park in the main parking lots or parking structure. Courtesy trams or buses will then transport Guests to the theme parks entrance Complex.

Parking for Guests with mobility disabilities—including those traveling with personal wheelchairs, electric scooters or other mobility devices—is identical to above. Transportation vehicles are able to carry you in your mobility device.

For further directions on parking options, Guests should inquire at the Parking Toll Booths.

At the Theme Parks

You should get a copy of the *Guide for Guests with Disabilities* for each theme park that you'll be visiting during your vacation. This is a brochure, which provides a detailed overview of services and facilities available for guests with disabilities at each location.

You can pick up a copy at all Guest Relations locations within the Esplanade area between the theme parks, your Disney Hotel front desk and concierge areas, and at Disney wheelchair/scooter rental locations.

This guide provides a detailed overview of the services and facilities available for guests with disabilities, including information about:

•Parking

•Companion restroom locations

•Accessible drinking fountain locations

•Auxiliary aids

•Telephone assistance

•Transportation facilities

•Specific attraction entrance and boarding procedures, as some attractions allow guests to remain in a wheelchair and some are transfer-accessible.

Guests with specific disability concerns can visit Guest Relations locations at both of the Disney Theme Parks for additional information and assistance.

Each theme park has a First Aid Station where you can store medications and spare oxygen tanks, or drop by in order to receive any needed assistance.

Trained Service Animals

It is important to note that Disney cast members are not permitted to take control of service animals. Guests with service animals should follow the same attraction entrance guidelines as those guests who use wheelchairs.

Each Theme Park allows guests to use backstage locations for service animal relief areas. Please consult your *Guide for Guests with Disabilities*, for specific information.

The Disability Access Service Card

Disneyland guests may obtain a Disability Access Service Card (DAS) from Guest Relations located at the front of each of the theme parks. Guest Relations Cast Members will discuss your individual needs with you. Based upon your specific needs DAS or other accommodations may be provided.

The Disability Access Service Card is intended for guests whose disability prevents them from waiting in a conventional queue environment. This service allows guests to schedule a return time that is comparable to the current queue wait for the given attraction. Once a return time is issued, guests are free to enjoy other theme park offerings such as meeting a character, grabbing a bite to eat, enjoying entertainment or even visiting another attraction until their listed return time. Return times are valid at any time after the listed time, there is no return window.

A Guest whose disability is based on the necessity to use a wheelchair or scooter does not need a DAS. Depending on the attraction, Guests utilizing a wheelchair or scooter will either wait in the standard queue or receive a return time at the attraction comparable to the current wait time.

Guests may only have one active return time. As soon as an outstanding attraction return time is redeemed, guests may receive a new return time for the same or different attraction.

Another member of your travel party can obtain a return time. However, the Guest in possession of DAS must board the attraction with his/her party.

This service can be used in addition to Disney's FastPass service.

The official guide to the Disability Access Service Card is available for download in PDF format. If you plan to request this accommodation, I highly recommend that you review the file thoroughly. (See the link at the end of the chapter)

Requests for the DAS accommodation are made in person at the theme park Guest Relations locations.

Types of Accommodations Available

Visual and Hearing Challenges

Disney offers many accommodations for guests with visual and hearing challenges

Some examples of these accommodations include:

•Assistive Listening systems

•Reflective Captioning

•Sign Language interpretation

•Text Typewriter telephones

•Handheld Captioning

•Video Captioning

•Audio Description devices

•Braille guidebooks

•Digital audio tour

Cognitive or Sensory Disabilities

Guests with cognitive or sensory disabilities, which make it difficult for the guest to wait in the traditional queue, are offered an alternate waiting environment via the DAS card.

Disney has created *A Recourse for Guests with Cognitive Disabilities including Autism Spectrum Disorder* which is available as PDF download. Some of the information in this guide is applicable to guests with Anxiety Disorders, PTSD, as well as sensory challenges, so even if the need is unrelated to Autism, it is worth a review. (See the link at the end of the chapter)

Mobility or Endurance Issues

Guests with mobility or endurance issues are offered the accommodation of wheelchair or ECV (scooter) rental if they do not already have their own assistive device and are offered the alternate entrance accommodation.

Guests are encouraged to utilize any of these accommodations in addition to the FastPass reservation system.

Wheelchairs and Electric Conveyance Vehicles

Wheelchairs and Electric Conveyance Vehicles (ECVs or "scooters") are available for rent from Disney on a daily basis in the Esplanade between the theme parks. Quantities are limited and they are available on a first-come-first-serve basis. Guests are permitted to bring their own mobility assistive devices.

Guests using wheelchairs or ECVs are provided the accommodation of alternate entrance. It should be noted that, due to safety regulations concerning the number of mobility-impaired guests that may utilize an attraction at one time, the wait for a particular attraction may actually be longer when using this accommodation. Options for boarding procedures are posted at the entrance to each attraction and may vary.

Scooter rental fees are $50 per day with an additional $20 refundable deposit. Wheelchairs are $12 per day with a refundable $20 deposit.

Physical Access

Most attractions, restaurants, shops and shows are accessible to all guests. In some cases, however, guests may need the assistance of a member of their party to fully utilize these areas. Also, at some attractions guests using wheelchairs may need to transfer from their wheelchairs onto an attraction vehicle. Disney Cast Members are not permitted to physically lift guests from wheelchairs. Disney recommends that guests who need assistance plan to visit with someone who can physically assist them, when necessary.

Prosthetic Devices

A Prosthesis Information Sheet is available at Guest Services. It will detail the restrictions in place for attractions for different types of prosthesis. These restrictions are different for each theme park. Cast Members operating attractions reserve the right to determine guest safety on an individual basis. The deciding factor appears to be whether or not the guest is able to be adequately restrained (on thrill rides) or is able to properly brace him-or herself, with or without the prosthesis.

Guests with Multiple Disabilities

If the guest has both a cognitive and a mobility disability, the guest should request both accommodations.

Multiple Guests with Disabilities

If there is more than one guest in a travel party with the need for accommodation with a Disability Access Service Card, it is highly recommended that each guest obtain his or her own card. This allows the guests to "split up" if needed and still make use of the accommodations.

Wrap Up

It is important for you to know that the American's With Disabilities Act prohibits Disney from requesting "proof" of disability or even a specific diagnosis. You are, of course, free to divulge your diagnosis if you so choose.

Disney Cast Members are discouraged from accepting "doctor's notes" that could support the guest's request for accommodation. This is to avoid the perception that Disney is requiring proof, which would be against Federal Law.

Please be aware that Cast Members are not health care providers and most likely will not have a clear understanding of your needs if you simply provide them with a medical diagnosis. Therefore, it is important that the guest or the guest's representative be able to clearly articulate the need.

While the DAS card is most commonly requested for use by guests with cognitive, sensory, or mental health challenges, there are other invisible medical challenges for which a guest may find the card useful. Again, it all depends upon the individual need. Some examples are:

•Medical conditions that may result in a rapid change in blood sugar, necessitating immediate treatment

•Medical conditions that may result in seizures, necessitating immediate treatment

•Medical conditions that make it difficult for a guest to wait in a traditional queue, yet preclude the guest from utilizing a wheelchair or ECV

If you require additional information about Services for guests with disabilities at the Disney Resorts, please call!!

Military Disney Tip

- Disney does a great job of accommodating those who need some assistance. Be sure to use both your DAS and FastPass together.

Resources

Disneyland Resort Disability information (407) 560-2547

Disneyland Services for Guests with Disabilities webpage, offers information and downloads: disneyland.disney.go/guest-services/guests-with-disabilities/

Ready for More?

In the next chapter I'm going to cover some tips, ideas, and guidelines for you, based upon my experiences touring Disney's parks since 1971.

12. Tips for Your Disneyland Vacation

What's This Chapter About?

My family and I have over 47 years of experience touring Disney's theme parks. This chapter contains some of our best tips to help you enjoy your vacation.

We've seen all the good and all of the "not so good" during our time in the parks which I'll share with you here.

This chapter also contains some "theme park etiquette." Things we've experienced that you should or shouldn't do. While mostly unintentional, these things can detract from your and other's theme park enjoyment.

The Basics

Sunscreen – Each of my Disneyland theme park day starts with an application of sunscreen before leaving my room. Even in the winter my face gets a coat. You are going to be in the sun 10 to 12 hours a day, don't risk a burn in the strong California sun, especially early in your vacation. The usually temperate weather can mask how strong the sun is even in the winter. When wearing out of the ordinary clothing, tank tops etc. consider applying sunscreen to areas not used to the sun!

Fitness Preparation – You may have just scored an excellent on your military fitness test, but that in no way assures you're in prefect shape for the 10 to 14 hour days of being mostly on your feet at a Disney park.

In the months prior to your vacation add in lots of walking (several hour plus walks a week), strengthening your core, and keeping your back and legs loose with stretching or yoga. Long days of walking many miles in the parks and lots of standing can wear on your lower half!

Shoes – I've seen all kinds of footwear at Disney! Everything from flip flops to huge wedge heels or stilettos. Just don't!

Because of the amount of time you will be spending on your feet (see the previous topic) you want good, broken in, comfortable, supportive shoes. Get a new pair of running, walking, or cross-fit shoes about a month before your trip. You do not want to be breaking them in at Disneyland! The newer gel or memory foam models are especially good.

Arrival and Departure Day Activities - Most likely you've spent most of your arrival day getting to Disneyland. You might feel that using a whole day of theme park tickets for just a few hours would be a waste. Or you've used up your park tickets during your stay and will be leaving for home in the afternoon. Here are some free or low cost things you can do to pass an evening or morning at Disneyland.

Chill out at your Resort Pool - Having just spent all day getting to Disneyland or getting ready for a full day going home can drain you. Perhaps you'd just like to spend some time relaxing at your own hotel. Take a dip in the pool or a soak in the hot tub.

Have a great meal - You've got to eat anyway so have a meal at one of Disney's great restaurants.

Go to Downtown Disney - Explore the Shops and wonderful dining options located there.

Take a tour of the Disney Resorts - The resorts are so beautiful, especially at Christmas. We love to check them out and see which one we'd like to stay at next. While touring you could have a drink in one of their lounges or grab a snack. Be sure to be on the lookout for Hidden Mickeys.

Mid-Day Breaks – during the busiest periods of the year, such as summer, Disneyland's parks are open for very long periods of time each day. For example the Disneyland Park can open at 6 am and close at 1 to 2 am. In the summer heat, staying through from opening to late at night is a recipe for disaster, sure to bring on the dreaded Disney melt down.

You can see it happen every day in the parks during the few hours after noon. Tired kids in sensory overload begin crying, screaming, falling down or just refusing to move and their tired, exasperated parents are just trying to contain the situation.

There is the famous quote "I paid a lot of money to come to Disney, you're going to have fun damn it!" Or the number two quote, "Why are you acting like this?"

A sure way to avoid this is the mid-day break. It's not just for the kids though.

Those who use the mid-day break will spend the morning in a park till about lunchtime. You can eat in the park or elsewhere after you leave. But the key is to get out! Temperatures will reach their peak about 2 or 3 pm. That's the time you want to be taking a nap in your air conditioned room or a having a dip in your resort's pool, not pounding the pavement in the theme park!

Once you get back to your resort you can grab some lunch, get your sweaty clothes off, have a nap (whether just the kids or everyone) and then head to the pool.

Later, about 5 or 6 pm, feeling refreshed you can head back to the same park, or a different one if you have a hopper ticket, and enjoy the evening as long as you'd like.

Dry clothes, socks, and maybe even shoes do a lot to improve your mood!

I highly recommend this! We did it when our kids were younger during family vacations and my wife and I still do it now that it is just the two of us.

Device Charging – an issue of modern life, that no one would have ever thought of, even when Disneyland's most recent theme park was built, is that the majority of theme park guests might one day need access to an electrical outlet to charge anything.

Disney's US theme parks have partnered with FuelRod to place portable charger sales and exchange stations in the theme parks and some resort hotels. The price for the FuelRods is $30.

At the Disneyland Resort they are located at:

Disneyland Park

- Main Street Locker Rental & Storage
- Starcade (near ATM)
- "it's a small world" Toy Shop
- Hungry Bear Restaurant (lower level)

Disney California Adventure Park

- Kingswell Camera
- Treasures in Paradise

Downtown Disney District

ESPN Zone

Disneyland Hotel

- Outside Business Center (Fantasy Tower)

Paradise Pier Hotel

- Hotel Lobby Area

You are better off buying and bringing your own cheaper, more powerful and versatile portable charge that you can buy on Amazon for as little as 14 to 35 bucks.

Personal Security, Safety, Severe Weather, Shelter in Place

Personal Security is a topic that should be near and dear to a military member/family's heart. Especially in today's world we should never let our guard down.

As you are enjoying your vacation it's easy to be totally focused in the moment and you should be. This is your time to de-stress. I just encourage you to keep a small bit of your attention on what's going on around you, just as you do when interacting with and in your local community.

The big threats are focused on our centers of government and worldwide trade, but Disney is a huge collection of people all in a small area. Just stay aware of your surroundings.

Rest assured that Disney has procedures and plans in place to deal with almost anything.

As you tour the parks you'll encounter local law enforcement officers and local/ Disney K-9 units at all the park entrances and uniformed Disney Security within the parks. But what you won't see are the many undercover Disney Security members that are roaming the parks for your protection.

Disney has procedures whether reactive or preventative, which I won't go into for dealing with and keeping their guests safe from many unlikely scenarios. Whether a criminal/terror situation or severe weather, Disney has shelter in place and evacuation plans. Some of these were put into play on September 11, 2001.

Theme Park Etiquette

This section discusses things that you should think about as you tour the Disney parks. I've been visiting the parks since 1971 and have experienced everything possible! Below are some things to avoid.

Being in a Disney park for the first time is a new, unfamiliar experience and you will most likely be in sensory overload while trying to find your way around. But there are multiple thousands of people all around you trying to enjoy their day as well. Study ahead of time so that you are familiar with layouts and what you want to do before you get there.

Stopping – Do not come to a dead stop while walking around Disneyland, whether to look at a park guide map, talk to someone in your party, fiddle with or load a stroller, scold a child, or show off the latest WWF move, especially if you are in an entrance or exit way, or a narrow walkway. There WILL be someone right behind you and someone behind them (often double or triple digits worth of people) who will be affected! Instead look around you and find an out of the way place to step off to prior to stopping.

Walking – Do not walk with your whole party abreast! Try to keep it to pairs. All people walk at different speeds and there will be people trying to get around you. Four to six people slowly walking abreast will create a huge traffic jam.

Walking – Always look where you are walking, never to the side or behind you while moving forward. Always walk forward not to the side or backwards.

Running – DON'T

Bag Check – Have all closed areas (zippers, Velcro, etc.) on your bag(s) open and ready for inspection prior to your turn! Those without bags can walk right through and wait on the other side of the bag check area for the person with the bag, this makes the lines shorter.

Cutting – Young kids have small bladders, it's a fact. Make sure you visit the bathroom prior to getting in line for an attraction. Don't send one person to get in line while the rest of the party visits the restroom. But if the need arises for a little one while in line it is understandable and acceptable (I think) to send one parent off with the child and then rejoin the party if you are comfortable with that.

Your whole party should wait in line! It is not fair to others to have one or two wait in line for the whole party while the rest shop, eat, or do anything else but stand in line and then join the ones who have been waiting as they near the ride boarding area.

Ordering in Quick Service Restaurants – All of Disneyland's Quick Service Restaurants have large overhead menus often with pictures. Often there is a closed line to one side where you can stand and check out the menu. Decide what you'd like to order prior to getting into the line to order, so that you will be ready to tell the cast member what you want when it is your turn. Do not keep both the cast member and those behind you waiting while you are deciding at the register.

Tables in Quick Service Restaurants – This particular item is a highly contested one, with firm proponents on each side. But these are my thoughts, which I humbly think are correct…

Imagine, ordering food for your family of four at a Disney park fast food location, after being served your party carries the 2 or 3 trays of food and drinks into the dining area to enjoy your meal and every single table is occupied. Not Fun! What is even worse though is that half of the tables are being saved by one person from a party that is still in line waiting to order their food.

If every party would get their food and then get their table the process would be smooth and due to the natural timing, tables would always be opening up as guests with their food were looking for one.

Also when you finish your food get up and move on. No long conversations over soda refills or coffee.

Smoking - If you are a smoker, please only smoke in the designated areas.

Strollers and Scooters – Please try to be considerate of the ankles of those around you. There are times and locations where quarters are very tight. Move slowly, don't try to zig-zag around or pass people. Keeping it slow and straight might take you a little longer to get where you are going, but everyone else around you will get there in one piece too.

Running with a Stroller – DON'T, REALLY DON'T

Parade/Show Viewing – Many families arrive well in advance of scheduled times for parades, shows, and fireworks presentations. They do so to ensure prime viewing locations. If you decline to spend the time waiting for prime real estate do not arrive late and push your children in front of, or crowd those who put in the time for that spot, so that your kids can see better.

On the other hand if you do have a prime spot, do not put your kids on your shoulders and block the view of those behind you.

Attraction/Show Seating – When seating the guests for the next showing/performance, a Disney cast member will be asking on the PA system that you "Move all the way to the end of a row (or three-quarters of the way when the show isn't full, and fill up every available seat." This is so that everyone coming into the seating area can get a seat without having to climb over those who plopped down in the middle of a row so that they could have the best view. If you don't want to sit on the far end, then don't be the first person to rush into a row. Hold back and let an appropriate number of people go into the row ahead of you.

Cell Phones – On silent in Attractions. No bright screens illuminating all around and behind you in dark shows!

Flash Photography – Don't do it on dark rides or shows!

Well that's about it. The above are just a collection of tips and pet peeves from my years in the parks. Being as mindful of those around you as possible will make not only your vacation, but everyone else's vacations go just a little bit smoother.

But also be mindful that there are those who haven't read all of this great advice and might not be up to speed!

So when you are moving forward in a line or mass of people at a reasonable speed and the family of four ahead of you stops dead in their tracks to look at their guide map (or do some WWF moves, yes this did happen to me), just shrug it off and continue enjoying the Happiest Place on Earth!

Ready for More?

Sadly it is time for us to begin wrapping this up. Next we'll do just that.

13. Wrapping It All Up

My family has so many great memories and experiences that were made at the Disney Resorts at many different stages of our lives. I write this as a retired E-9 who often enjoys going to going to Disney with just my wife, but in year's past we've gone with our children, when they were adults, teens, tweens, and young to very young kids. There has always been a plethora of things to do and see for each stage of our family's life. In late 2018 we will take our first trip to Walt Disney World with our new grand baby. There has always been a plethora of things to do and see for each stage of our family's life.

There is a Disney experience for every budget. Going now, or recently as I did before I retired is certainly at a different price point than how we did it as a young E-5's family staying at Walt Disney World's Shades of Green or off property. But that's the beauty of Disney; with all the various options you can have a fantastic vacation no matter your pay grade!

I want to touch again, as I did in the introduction on what an immersive experience Disneyland can be. Disney is very good at what it does in this respect and it is a win-win. I firmly believe that Disney's Parks are one of the best, if not the best places on earth for military families to take time out from their hectic stressful lives that the majority of the US population does not understand, to de-stress and just be together in a place where nothing else matters. For a time to just be together, experiencing new and wonderful things.

My thanks go out to the Walt Disney Company for their firm support of the military community, which has been at an all-time high these last nine years with the Disney Armed Forces Salute and the Heroes Work Here military hiring program. It has been a pleasure and my honor to work with my Disney contacts over the years, providing input from the military perspective and being able to get some positive changes instituted.

And I'm thankful for you, the reader! Thankful for your service to our nation and also for the understanding and sacrifice of all the military spouses and children! It truly is a greater calling. Thanks so much for the purchase of this book; I hope that it was truly useful to you!

Be sure to check out my website, MilitaryDisneyTips.com, there you will find plenty more information and all of the new and newsworthy things that affect our community as well as updates to things that might have changed since publication.

Also if you wouldn't mind, please drop by Amazon by using the following link to leave a review for this book. Your review helps the book gain visibility, so that others can find it on Amazon and helps them in making their decision to purchase this book. It does not matter if you purchased the book on Amazon or not, all reviews are accepted.

disneylandformilitary.com/review

Thanks and See ya real soon,
Steve Bell
Washington Township, Ohio, October 2018

Other Books by Steve:

Walt Disney World for Military Families: wdwformilitary.com

The Essential Guide to Shades of Green: shadesofgreenguide.com

About the Author

Steve Bell is widely recognized as THE Military Disney Discount Expert. With the knowledge gained in 47 years of touring Disney parks and three years working on the front lines at Walt Disney World's Magic Kingdom, he has spent 29 years helping fellow military members plan for and save on their Disney vacations.

Steve is the founder of the hugely popular MilitaryDisneyTips.com website. He recently retired from the Air Force after 31 years of service, with tours as a Career Enlisted Aviator with over 7000 hours heavy jet time, a Civil Search and Rescue Duty Officer, and an aircraft mechanic.

Besides sharing Disney information with the military community, Steve continuously advocates on behalf of his brethren with Disney to correct poor military discount policy and expand discounts where possible.

Made in the USA
Lexington, KY
08 February 2019